Volume 3

FOX 13
TAMPA BAY

ONE TANK TRIPS®
WITH BILL MURPHY
Off The Beaten Path

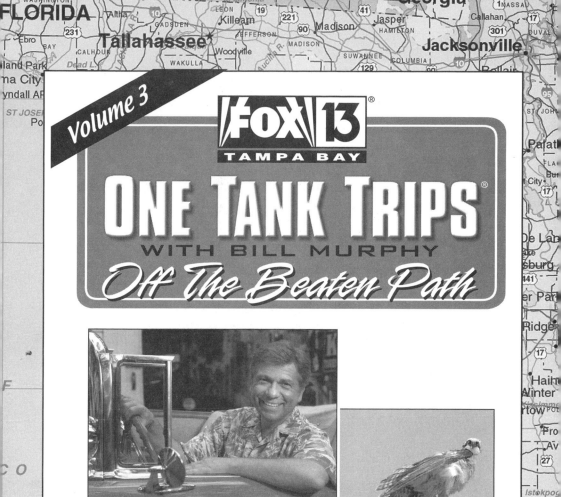

D0115510

Seaside
Publishing

Publisher
Seaside Publishing
Frank & Karen Nabozny

Design & Illustration
Kevin Coccaro
James Wahl

Editorial Staff
Fred. W. Wright Jr.
Nichol Fuller, Mike House,
Philip Metlin, Bill Murphy, Carrie Schroeder

Additional copies of this book may be ordered by calling:
1-888-ONE-TANK (663-8265)

Or you may write the Publisher at:

Seaside
Publishing
1395 Belcher Rd., Palm Harbor, FL 34683

Visit our Web site and order online at: **famousflorida.com**
E-mail: **famousflorida@famousflorida.com**

ISBN: 0-9760555-0-3

Library of Congress Catalog Number: 2004095672

Cover Photography—Front: Bill Murphy at Heritage Village in Largo. 1955 Chevy BelAir
convertible courtesy of P.J.'s Classic Autos (Trip 32). **Photo by Alex McKnight;** (© WTVT FOX13).
Back—Clockwise left to right: Bill kayaking at the Little Manatee River (© Little Manatee
River Canoe Outpost); big smiles at Old McMicky's farm (© Old McMicky's Farm); a content
tiger at Big Cat Rescue (© Jamie Veronica); a beautiful spring bloom at the Florida
Botanical Gardens (© Florida Botanical Gardens); Bill Murphy enjoying an old classic,
Photo by Alex McKnight; (© WTVT FOX13).

Interior Photography—All photos copyright of WTVT FOX13 unless indicated otherwise.

Title page photos—Top to bottom: Bill driving the old '55 (© WTVT FOX13); a watchful Osprey
at Weedon Island (© WTVT FOX13); quiet serenity on the Hillsborough River
(© Hillsborough River Canoe Escape).

Special Sales: Bulk purchases (12+ copies) of *FOX13's One Tank Trips With Bill Murphy—Off The
Beaten Path* are available to bookstores, gift shops, special groups, distributors, and wholesalers
at quantity discounts. For more information call: **1-888-ONE-TANK (663-8265),**
or write to: Seaside Publishing, 1395 Belcher Rd., Palm Harbor, FL 34683

While we have been very careful to ensure the accuracy of the information in this guide,
time brings change and, consequently, the publisher cannot accept responsibility for errors
which may occur. All prices and opening times are based on information given to us
at press time. All prices are quoted without tax. Most trip directions are given with Tampa
as a starting point. **Admission fees and hours may change, so be sure to call ahead.**
Most trips have facilities for the handicapped, but do call ahead to confirm.
We welcome your comments and suggestions for future editions.

No maps, illustrations or other portions of this guide may be reproduced in
any form without written permission from the publisher and WTVT FOX13.

Dedication

This one I dedicate to my co-workers at FOX13.
The hardest working and most talented
bunch I've ever known. No wonder we're
the best station in the country!
And to my love, my daughter Jessica Leigh.

Acknowledgments

Special recognition belongs to:

Robert Linger, Vice President & General Manager

Phil Metlin, News Director

Mike House, Creative Services Director

James Wahl, Design Director

Kevin Coccaro, Graphic Designer

Rick Hardman, Chief Photographer

Luke Marquis, Video Editor

Carrie Schroeder, Promotion/Publicity Manager

Nan Grable, Executive Assistant

And

Each and Every Member of the FOX13 Team

Also

Carolyn Forrest, Vice President, FTS

The Staff at Seaside Publishing

Table Of Contents

Table Of Contents

Florida Map

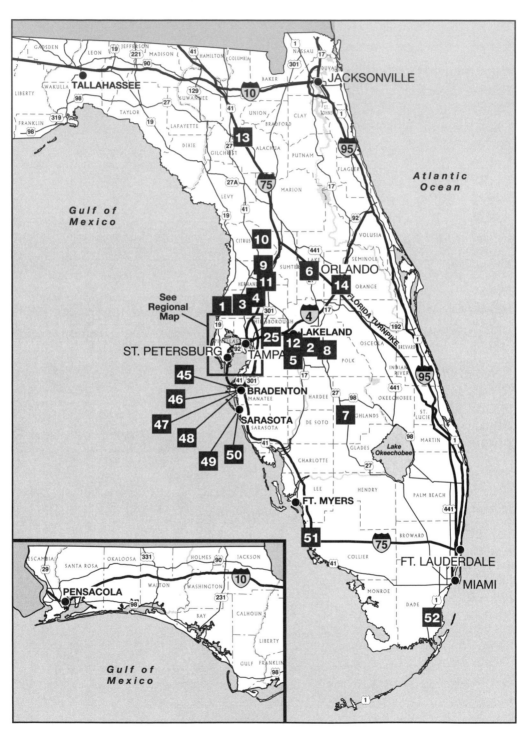

Regional Map

One Tank Trips
CENTRAL FLORIDA
1 Cotee River Boats
2 Elmo & Linda's Magical Shady Oaks Café
3 Famous Treasures Antiques
4 Florida Estates Winery
5 Frank Lloyd Wright's "Child Of The Sun"
6 House Of Presidents & Citrus Tower
7 Lake Placid–City Of Murals
8 Lake Wales Arts Center
9 Nobleton Withlacoochee Canoe Trip
10 Old Courthouse Heritage Museum
11 Old Florida Tourism At Boyette's Grove
12 Polk County Museum Of Art
13 Retired Horse Farm Experience
14 Rock & Roll Museum

WEST CENTRAL FLORIDA
Hillsborough County
15 Big Cat Rescue
16 Camp Bayou
17 DolphinQuest Ecotour
18 Hillsborough River Canoe Escape
19 In The Breeze Horse Camp
20 Jibac Gallery
21 Little Manatee Canoe Outpost
22 Lowry Park Zoo River Odyssey Ecotour
23 Manatee Viewing Center
24 Old McMicky's Farm
25 Plant City Historic Trains Tours
26 S.S. American Victory
27 Sharks!
28 Tampa Police Museum
29 Ybor City Walking Tour

Pinellas County
30 Caladesi Island State Park
31 Capt. Bill's Yacht Cruises
32 Classic Autos At P.J.'s
33 Dunedin Main Street
34 Florida Botanical Gardens
35 Gulf Beaches Historical Museum
36 Gulf Coast Museum Of Art

37 H&R Trains
38 K. Kringle's Christmas Shoppe
39 Leepa-Rattner Museum Of Art
40 Packinghouse Art Gallery
41 St. Petersburg Museum Of History
42 Science Center Of Pinellas County
43 Weedon Island Preserve
44 World Of Disc Golf

Manatee County
45 DeSoto National Memorial
46 Manatee Village Historical Park
47 Sea Hagg Nautical Oddities
48 Village Of The Arts

Sarasota County
49 Pelican Man Bird Sanctuary
50 Sarasota Ever-Glides Tour

SOUTHWEST FLORIDA
51 The Teddy Bear Museum

SOUTHEAST FLORIDA
52 Coral Castle

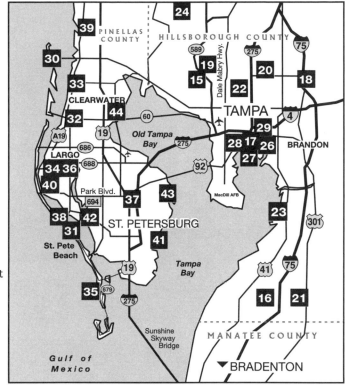

Still On Sale!

For years, **FOX13**'s Bill Murphy has been roaming the state searching for unique and exciting places you can visit on one tank of gas.

Both the original **"One Tank Trips"** book and volume two **"More One Tank Trips"** have been best sellers in Florida. Each book contains 52 destinations—one for every weekend of the year.

Whether you are new to the Sunshine State, or have lived here all your life, you'll find all of our **"One Tank Trips"** books to be the perfect guides to places that are truly Florida treasures. Each guide is packed with information including how to get there, admission prices, hours of operation and web site addresses. These handy books belong in every adventurer's glove compartment.

To purchase **"One Tank Trips,"** **"More One Tank Trips"** or additional copies of **"One Tank Trips – Off The Beaten Path,"** visit Bay Area bookstores, log onto **www.wtvt.com** or call **1-888-ONE-TANK (663-8265)**.

A Word From FOX13

Bill Murphy's wonderful insights and keen eye for family fun destinations have made his **"One Tank Trip"** segments on **FOX13 News** a huge hit.

Viewer calls to **FOX13** following the airing of these segments eventually led to the Florida best selling book **"One Tank Trips with Bill Murphy."** A second highly successful book, **"*More* One Tank Trips with Bill Murphy,"** followed.

The continued enthusiastic response we get each time a **"One Tank Trip"** segment airs on **FOX13,** and the many pleas from fans at Bill's book signings, inspired this, our third book.

Inside this guide are 52 new educational and entertaining destinations across our state that are "Off the Beaten Path" of the usual Florida theme parks.

A number of people at **FOX13** are responsible for helping to put together this new book. I hope you'll have as much fun learning about these new adventures as we have in compiling this guide.

Enjoy the book and be sure to watch **FOX13 News** for even more **"One Tank Trips."**

Robert W. Linger

Robert W. Linger
Vice President & General Manager
WTVT FOX13 Television

About Bill

Bill Murphy is a veteran TV news reporter and anchor. He has spent more than 20 years in broadcasting in the Tampa Bay area. Bill is most well known for his series of feature reports, **"One Tank Trips."** These unique segments highlight one-of-a-kind destinations you can reach on one tank of gas or less.

After moving to the Tampa Bay area, Bill became host of "Murphy in the Morning." This popular talk show received an Emmy nomination in 1991. Since then, Bill has been anchoring **FOX13**'s **"Good Day Tampa Bay"** on **FOX13**, the most successful morning newscast in Florida. Bill also anchors **FOX13**'s **"Good Day Tampa Bay"** Saturday and Sunday mornings as well as presenting his weekly "Murphy at the Movies" reviews.

Before he came to Florida, Bill's broadcast career included seven years as an anchor at KSBW-TV in Monterey, Calif., and stints in Seattle, Palm Springs and Los Angeles.

Bill has hosted MDA and Easter Seal telethons and The Miss Florida Teen USA Pageant. He was named "Favorite Television Personality" and his show, "Murphy in the Morning," was voted "Best Local Talk Show" by *Tampa Bay Magazine*.

In November 1999, **FOX13** decided to turn Bill's **"One Tank Trip"** segments into a series of books. The first volume quickly became a bestseller in Florida and was followed by the release of volume two, **"More One Tank Trips"** in 2001. Thousands of fans have turned out for more than 100 autographing sessions at bookstores, gift shops, specialty stores, libraries and even Air Force bases.

When he's not watching the gas gauge and driving off in search of another intriguing **"One Tank Trip,"** Bill likes to spend time with his daughter. He also enjoys reading, tennis, handball, in-line skating and disc golf.

We're Taking You Off The Beaten Path!

Many moons ago (it seems) I was asked if I'd like to do a travel series for **FOX13**. We'd call it **"One Tank Trips"** and it would feature interesting and fun destinations for all the family. A few weeks later, we headed out to our first destination. It was a place I went camping, Hillsborough River State Park. When we did that story, I remember thinking to myself, "Where will I go next?" For a while, I thought I'd never find anyplace else! Now after several years, hundreds of trips and three books, we're still discovering and enjoying Florida fun spots.

Sometimes people will ask me to define the "One Tank" in **"One Tank Trip."** Okay, a few years ago, we filled up at the gas station down the street from **FOX13** and made it all the way to Key Largo with a quarter of a tank to spare! We really did. So, as far as I'm concerned, "One Tank Country" is most of the wonderful Sunshine State.

So, my adventure continues and I sure hope you'll have as much fun enjoying these places as I did finding them.

I would like to ask you a favor. **Please, please, please** call ahead before you take off on any of your own **"One Tank Trips."** Sometimes places close for a day or two. Sometimes the weather is not good. Sometimes hours or prices change. It will be well worth your while to check ahead before you buckle up. That way, you won't say mean things about me when you get there and it's not what you expected! :)

Who knows? Maybe I'll see you on the road. Oh, and don't forget to contact me with your "One Tank" ideas.

Happy trails!

Bill Murphy

Volume 3

FOX 13
TAMPA BAY

ONE TANK TRIPS
WITH BILL MURPHY

Off The Beaten Path

Cotee River Boats

FLOATING UP—AND DOWN—A LAZY RIVER

Cotee River Boats

A pontoon boat awaits your arrival.

Cotee River Boats

The Trip

In case you didn't know, there are 1,711 rivers and streams in the state of Florida. My quest is to "One Tank" each and every one of them. This trip took us to Pasco County.

What To See

The Cotee is a 20-mile-long blackwater stream. Its Seminole-Creek Indian name translates to "The River Where Canoes Are Made." While we didn't see anyone making canoes, there were plenty to see on the water. Besides canoes you can also rent pontoon boats or johnboats. If your heart's set on a canoe, you can rent one next door. The cost depends on how big of a boat you want and how long you want to be on the river. We opted for the user-friendly pontoon boat, a lazy way to see the Pithlachascotee River or "Cotee" for short.

Other Highlights

We're told that some famous names spent time in this neck of the woods and had homes on the river. Among them were Johnny and June Carter Cash, Shirley Temple and the notorious Al Capone. If you're looking for a place to snack on the river, stop by The Crab Shack. You can spot it by the big shark in front.

5448 BAYLEA AVENUE
PORT RICHEY, FL 34668
(727) 841-7664

Admission: *Boat rentals range from $70 to $225 depending on length of trip and style of boat.*

Hours: *Open Tuesday through Sunday, 9 a.m. to 5 p.m. Closed Monday.*

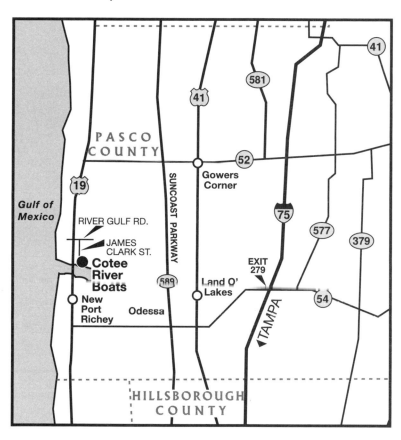

Directions

From Tampa, take Interstate 75 north to New Port Richey/ S.R. 54 (Exit #279). Turn left and go west. Continue for about 18 miles until you hit U.S. 19 North. Turn right and go north for about 5 miles. You will cross a bridge. Immediately over the bridge, take first right onto River Gulf Road. After about 20 feet, turn right onto James Clark Street. Go one block. Cotee Boat Rentals is at the southwest corner of James Clark Street and Baylea Avenue.

"WE OPTED
FOR THE
USER-FRIENDLY
PONTOON BOAT."

Central Florida

Elmo & Linda's Magical Shady Oaks Café

FOOD AND SLEIGHT OF HAND— ALL FOR THE SAME PRICE

Linda and the always magical Elmo.

Elmo & Linda's Shady Oaks Café

The Trip

This magical place to dine can be found in the heart of Winter Haven. Elmo and Linda have been serving up a combination of good eats and sleight of hand here since 1998. While the food is excellent, Elmo is certainly the star of the show. His card and magic tricks will amaze and entertain you.

What To See

You can eat inside, but I discovered the best experience is dining outside in a beautiful setting under the big shady oaks. What's good? Everything! The menu is full of "playing card-themed" delights like the Dealer's Choice, One-Eyed Jack or the Full House. If you get a chance, try the "SOS," which is the Shady Oaks Special. One of my favorites is the Stuffed Elmo, which is meat loaf stuffed with Swiss cheese and ham. Come for the food and the fun. Elmo's 20-plus years of magical expertise and experience are willingly shared with customers.

Other Highlights

I enjoyed watching other people as Elmo did his card tricks. One of his favorites involves a playing card held by a clip hanging around his neck. Be sure to ask him to perform it for you. By the way, if you want to do a disappearing act, items on the menu are also available for takeout.

132 Avenue "B" SW
Winter Haven, FL 33880
(863) 292-0234

Central Florida

Admission: *Free, but they suggest you call ahead for reservations. Prices on menu items vary.*

Hours: *Open Monday through Friday, 11 a.m. to 3 p.m. as well as 5 p.m. to 9 p.m. Friday. Closed Saturday, Sunday and the month of August.*

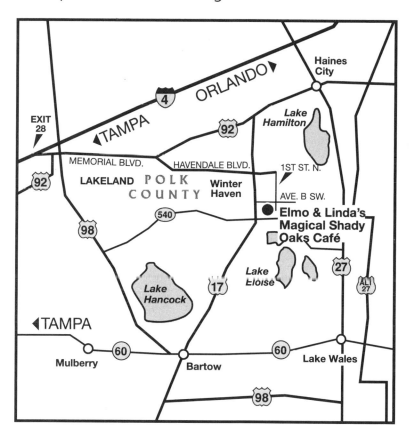

Directions

From Tampa, take Interstate 4 east to Memorial Boulevard (Exit #28). Take Memorial Boulevard through Lakeland. (It will turn into U.S. 92.) Go right onto Havendale Boulevard and continue past S.R. 17, as it becomes Avenue "T" NW. The next traffic light will be First Street North. Turn right and stay on First Street North past Central Avenue. Turn right on Avenue "B" SW and the café is on the left.

"WHERE MEAT LOAF MEETS MAGIC!"

Central Florida

Famous Treasures
Antiques
WHERE THE PAST IS TREASURED

A real "Coke Classic."

Joe Espi

This treasure is not buried.

Joe Espi

The Trip
If you like hunting for hidden treasures, this Land O' Lakes store is a delightful discovery. This place is full of unusual and hard-to-find antiques and collectibles.

What To See
The exploring adventure begins even before you walk through the door. You'll find a 1928 Ford F-5 truck parked out front. It's the first one Coca-Cola purchased from the automaker. Inside, it's easy to get lost among the estimated 4,000 items on display. Everywhere you turn, something is sure to catch your eye. I was amazed at the variety of antique china, silverware and even old military uniforms. The discoveries here range in price from a buck or two all the way up to $100,000 for a rare Babe Ruth lobby card. They tell me it's the only one in existence.

Other Highlights
If you have a particular collectible you're looking for, be sure to ask. Many of the items here are of museum quality, so even if you end up just looking, it's well worth the trip.

4312 Land O' Lakes Blvd.
Land O' Lakes, FL 34639
(813) 996–1787

Admission: *Free*

Hours: *Monday through Saturday, 9 a.m. to 5 p.m. Closed Sunday and major holidays.*

www.famoustreasures.com

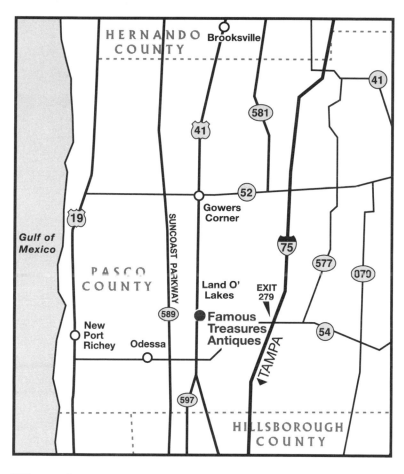

Directions
From Tampa, take Interstate 75 north to New Port Richey/ S.R. 54 (Exit #279). Turn left and go west on S.R. 54 to U.S. 41. Take a right on U.S. 41 and go north about two miles. The store is on the right side of the street, with a big neon sign.

"A 'ONE TANK' TREASURE."

Florida Estates Winery
ENJOYING THE GRAPES OF THE VINE

Central Florida

Exploring the tastes of some of Florida's best wines.

Florida Estates Winery

The Trip
This "One Tank" takes you to Pasco County wine country for a taste of Florida's finest. Much to my surprise, I discovered a 10-acre vineyard and winery right in the middle of a huge cattle ranch.

What To See
The owners of this establishment converted an old ranch bunkhouse into a busy winery. Tours of the vineyard and information about the wine making process are free and yes, there are free samples. The tasting room offers nine selections, seven with the Florida Estates label and two from their sister winery in Fort Myers. Some of these wines are made with 100 percent Florida grapes, others with a combination of Florida and California grapes.

Other Highlights
Each Saturday, from 11 a.m. to 3 p.m., there is a more elaborate wine tasting for $3.50. In addition to the folks from Florida Estates, several other wine vendors participate. Entertainment is usually provided by a live band. I recommend packing a picnic lunch. Just stretch out under a beautiful canopy of oaks and enjoy the festivities.

25241 State Road 52
Land O' Lakes, FL 34639
(813) 996-2113

Admission: *Free. Special wine tastings, $3.50.*

Hours: *Open daily, 11 a.m. to 5 p.m.*

www.floridaestateswines.com

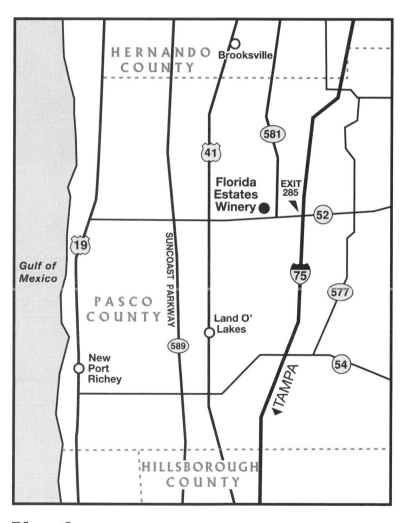

Directions

From Tampa, take Interstate 75 north. Turn left at S.R. 52/
San Antonio/Dade City (Exit #285) and go west. Go 4
miles. Winery is on the right.

"SOMETHING
TO 'WINE'
ABOUT."

Frank Lloyd Wright's "Child Of The Sun"

THE "WRIGHT" WAY TO SEE ARCHITECTURE

Central Florida

Florida Southern College

A bust of the famed architect oversees the Visitor's Center that honors his 14 on-campus designs.

Florida Southern College

The Trip

Florida Southern College in Lakeland is the home of the largest collection of Frank Lloyd Wright buildings in the world. In the mid-1930s, the college president felt the school needed to grow, so he asked the famous architect for help. As Wright toured the grounds, he said he envisioned the buildings rising "out of the ground, and into the light, a child of the sun." During construction, Wright would often show up carrying a walking stick and wearing a flowing cape and a beret.

What To See

There are 14 buildings in this magnificent collection. Self-guided tours can be done at your own pace. Make sure you wear a comfortable pair of walking shoes. The best way to start your journey is by picking up a map at the Visitor's Center. Each remarkable structure has its own story. Keep an eye out for "The Bicycle Rack in the Sky." That's what they call the Wright-designed Pfeiffer Chapel because of the wrought iron at its top. The fabled architect liked to use organic material in his creations when possible. The concrete block for the chapel was made from coquina shells from St. Augustine and sand from Davenport, Fla. Strolling through this beautiful college campus is a wonderful way to spend a day.

Other Highlights

The buildings are viewable without checking in with the Visitor's Center, but I highly recommend getting a map. For a small fee, guided tours are conducted on Thursdays or by appointment.

FLORIDA SOUTHERN COLLEGE
111 LAKE HOLLINGSWORTH DRIVE
LAKELAND, FL 33801
(863) 680-4553

Admission: Free. Guided tours are $5 for adults, $2.50 for seniors; children free.

Hours: Visitor's Center open Monday through Friday, 10 a.m. to 4 p.m.; Saturday, 10 a.m. to 2 p.m.; Sunday, 2 p.m. to 4 p.m.

www.flsouthern.edu/fllwctr/history.htm

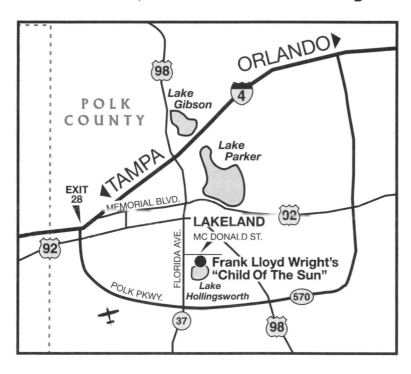

Directions

From Tampa, take Interstate 4 east to Memorial Boulevard (Exit #28). Take Memorial Boulevard into Lakeland. (It will turn into U.S. 92.) Turn right and go south on Florida Avenue. Turn left at McDonald Street. Florida Southern College campus is ahead on the right. Go to the end of the first parking lot. Follow signs to the Frank Lloyd Wright Visitor's Center on the right.

"AN AMAZING
COLLECTION
OF THE
"WRIGHT"
STUFF."

House Of Presidents & Citrus Tower

A PLACE TO STAND TALL AND FEEL PRESIDENTIAL

The nearby Citrus Tower offers a unique view of Central Florida.

Presidential statues welcome visitors.

The Trip

This "One Tank" is truly a two-for-one excursion! The House of Presidents and Citrus Tower are located right next to each other near Clermont, Florida.

What To See

First, we'll start with the House of Presidents. This amazing collection honors our past and present leaders of America. The displays are realistic, well planned and well worth the visit. One of the first things you'll find is an animated diorama depicting the building of the White House under the direction of George Washington. You will also find exact replicas of Abe Lincoln's face and hands that were made back in 1860. There's even a miniature Oval Office and an elaborate room where you'll feel like the guest of honor at a state dinner.

Towering over the House of Presidents, you'll find a 226-foot tall concrete structure called the Citrus Tower. Built in 1956 on one of the highest hills in Florida, the tower contains 5 million pounds of concrete, stands 22 stories tall and was built to withstand hurricane force winds. The glass-enclosed observation deck, accessed by elevator, offers a view of hundreds of spring-fed lakes. On a clear day, you can see parts of eight counties as well as Walt Disney World. One last thing, bring a penny with you. You'll find out why when you get to the top!

Other Highlights

Don't forget to browse through "Lilly's" gift shop. It's full of unique citrus-oriented souvenirs.

House Of Presidents
123 U.S. 27 N., Clermont, FL 34711
(352) 394-2836

Admission: *$9.95 for adults; $4.95 for children 5-11.*

Hours: *Open daily 9 a.m. to 5 p.m. Closed Thanksgiving and Christmas.*

Citrus Tower
141 U.S. 27 N., Clermont, FL 34711
(352) 394-4061

Admission: *$3.50 for adults; $1 for children 3-15. Under 3, free.*

Hours: *Monday through Thursday, 9 a.m. to 6 p.m. Friday and Saturday, 9 a.m. to 9 p.m. Closed Sunday, Thanksgiving and Christmas.*

www.citrustower.com

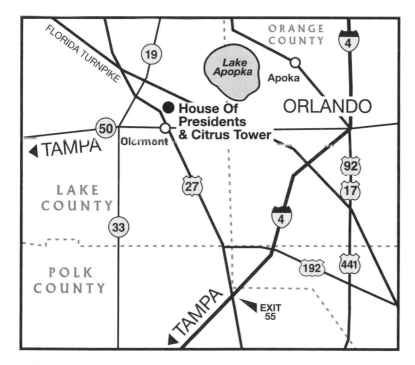

Directions

From Tampa, take Interstate 4 east to U.S. 27 (Exit #55). Turn left and go north about 20 miles. Cross over S.R. 50. About three-fourths of a mile north, on the right, you will see Citrus Tower. The House of Presidents is on the same property.

"Presidential
And
Picturesque."

TRIP
7

Lake Placid– City Of Murals

WHERE THE MURALS ARE
WORTH A THOUSAND VISITS

*Every mural has a story, told
in rich detail and colors.*

The Trip

If a picture really is worth a thousand words, then this pretty community requires an entire dictionary! Called "The City of Murals," Lake Placid's unique artwork began to appear in 1993. Now about 40 remarkable murals grace this town of 1,600.

What To See

What to see are the murals, of course! Scattered through town, take your time enjoying each of them. They all have a special story. Many of the murals come complete with sound effects like the one called "Train Depot." I marveled at the sound of the approaching locomotive and the clanging of the crossing bells! You can feel the sense of great pride the folks here have for their public artwork.

Other Highlights

Check out the town's trash cans. One looks like a small car, another a house. There's even one that looks like the town jail. All are extremely colorful and fun. Stop by the chamber of commerce to see the murals in miniature. Lake Placid is also the caladium capital of the world and hosts the annual "Caladium Festival," a three-day celebration in August.

LAKE PLACID
CHAMBER OF COMMERCE
18 N. OAK AVENUE
LAKE PLACID, FL 33852
(863) 465-4331

Admission: *Free*

Hours: *The murals are outdoors and can be seen anytime. Renderings for most murals are in the chamber of commerce building, open 9 a.m. to 4 p.m. Monday through Friday; closed Saturday, Sunday and holidays.*

www.visitlakeplacidflorida.com

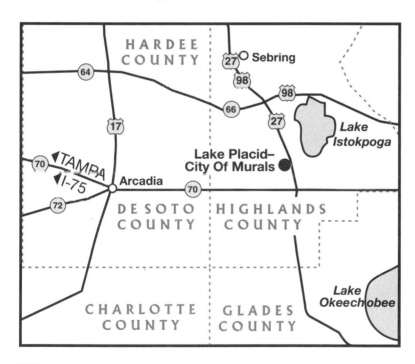

Directions

From Tampa, take Interstate 75 south through Bradenton to S.R. 70 (Exit #217). Turn left and go east on S.R. 70 to U.S. 27. Turn left and go north. The chamber of commerce is about 10 miles ahead at the intersection of Interlake and U.S. 27. Turn left. The chamber is in the old post office building (with blue awning).

"YOU OUGHTTA BE IN PICTURES!"

TRIP 8
Lake Wales Arts Center
A WELL-KEPT SECRET WORTH DISCOVERING

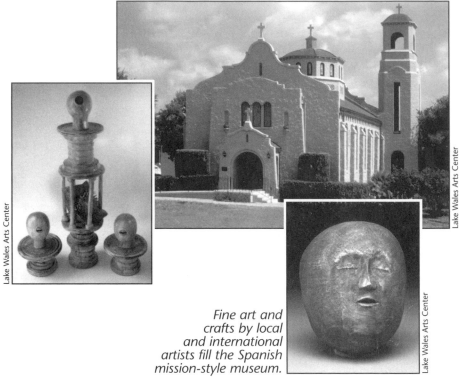

Fine art and crafts by local and international artists fill the Spanish mission-style museum.

Lake Wales Arts Center

Lake Wales Arts Center

Lake Wales Arts Center

The Trip

The Lake Wales Arts Center is housed in a beautiful old church that's listed on the National Register of Historic Places. With this trip you get a taste of the old and the new!

What To See

The Holy Spirit Catholic Church was built in 1927. It is a spectacular example of Spanish mission-style architecture. Now the building is home to a wide variety of the visual and performing arts. Pop, jazz, Broadway and the classics all have a home on stage here. In the galleries, the works of artists from around the state are on display. Exhibits are changed regularly so you'll want to make this a repeat "One Tank." Be sure to check the center's web site to find out the latest offerings.

Other Highlights

The historic church has beautiful stained-glass windows and stone carvings on the walls. There's also a gift shop filled with souvenirs including reproductions and postcards of the art you'll see in the galleries.

1099 State Road 60 E.
Lake Wales, FL 33853
(863) 676-8426

Admission: *Free. Donations accepted.*

Hours: *Open Monday through Friday, 9 a.m. to 4 p.m.; Saturday, 10 a.m. to 4 p.m.; Sunday, 1 p.m. to 4 p.m. Closed on weekends June through August.*

www.lakewalesartscenter.org

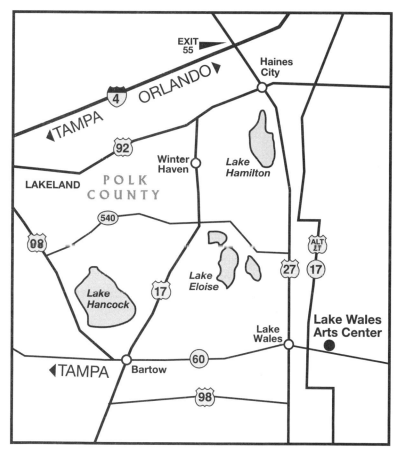

Directions

From Tampa, take Interstate 4 east to U.S. 27 (Exit #55). Go south on U.S. 27 to S.R. 60. Turn left and go east on S.R. 60. Arts Center is located in an old Catholic church on the left. Turn left onto 11th Street for parking.

"ONE OF THE MOST STRIKING EXAMPLES OF SPANISH MISSION-STYLE ARCHITECTURE."

Central Florida

Nobleton Withlacoochee Canoe Trip

A RIVER ADVENTURE—AT YOUR OWN PACE

Nobleton Canoe Rental

It's easy to spot this destination. Just look for the canoe.

Paddling my way along the Withlacoochee River.

Nobleton Canoe Rental

The Trip

Canoeing on the winding Withlacoochee is a great way to relax and take in the simple beauty of unspoiled Florida. Be sure to give yourselves plenty of time.

What To See

Just 12 miles north of Brooksville, this boating adventure is one you won't want to miss. There is a variety of paddling trips ranging anywhere from two to five hours. You're dropped off upstream and picked up downstream. If you'd like to go, but don't want to paddle, you can rent a canoe with a motor. You can also rent fishing boats, pontoon boats or even take a ride on an airboat!

Other Highlights

There are limited overnight accommodations available. If you enjoy cycling, you can rent bicycles to take advantage of the nearby "Rails to Trails" paved pathway. It winds through the Withlacoochee State Forest.

29196 Lake Lindsey Road
Nobleton, FL 34661
(800) 783-5284

Admission: Canoe rentals are $35 for a two-seater, $40 for a three-seater. A trolling motor and battery can be rented for an extra $35 per canoe.

Hours: Open daily, 8 a.m. to dark.

www.nobletoncanoes.com

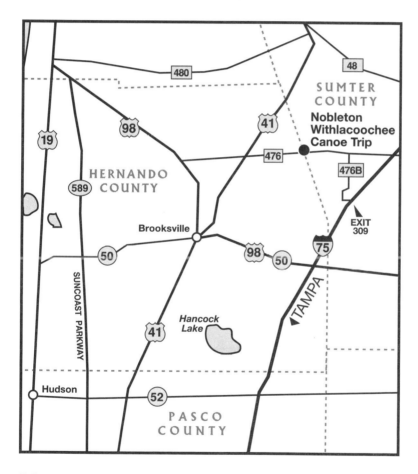

Directions
From Tampa, take Interstate 75 north to Exit #309. Take C.R. 476B north to C.R. 476. Turn left and go west. Entrance is on right immediately after crossing small bridge that is the Sumter/Hernando county line.

"ROW, ROW, ROW YOUR BOAT."

Central Florida

Old Courthouse Heritage Museum

WHERE HISTORY HAS BEEN RESTORED

Old Florida heritage is honored at the Old Courthouse, both inside and out.

The Trip

The pride of Citrus County can be found at One Courthouse Square in Inverness. The Old Courthouse Heritage Museum is a magnificent example of turn-of-the-century public architecture. But it's not all "ancient" history. There's actually an Elvis connection. Talk about a courthouse that rocks!

What To See

Several viewing areas await visitors in this grand old building. The John Murray Davis Gallery hosts exhibits from around the world and changes from time to time. You can spend as much time as you like exploring the halls of this historic place. A $2.5 million, 7-year restoration was completed here in October of 2000. That's quite a contrast to the $6,000 it originally cost to build it in 1912. Preservation architects have restored many of the artifacts inside as well. You can find documents more than a hundred years old, including stark reminders of the injustices of segregation.

Other Highlights

Who would guess there would be an Elvis link to this old building? In 1961, Elvis filmed part of the movie "Follow that Dream" in the courtroom. You can find rare video copies of the film in the Judge E.C. May Gallery, which is also the museum store. If you get a chance, give yourself some extra time to explore nearby shops and restaurants.

ONE COURTHOUSE SQUARE INVERNESS, FL 34450 (352) 341-6429

Central Florida

Admission: Free

Hours: Monday through Friday, 8 a.m. to 5 p.m.; Saturday, 10 a.m. to 2 p.m. Guided tours available Monday through Friday, 10 a.m. to 4 p.m. Closed Sunday.

www.cccourthouse.org

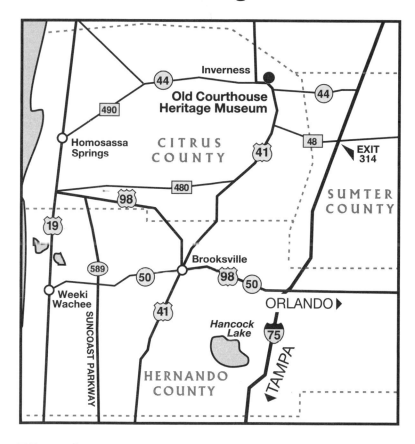

Directions

From Tampa, take Interstate 75 north to C.R. 48/Dade Battlefield exit (Exit #314). Turn left (under the overpass) and go west to U.S. 41. Turn right and go north about 7 miles to Inverness. The second traffic light, South Apopka, is the town square. Courthouse is on the northeast corner.

"THERE'S EVEN AN ELVIS CONNECTION."

Old Florida Tourism
At Boyette's Grove
THE FLAVOR OF YEARS GONE BY

Central Florida

Boyette's Grove

Boyette's Grove

A variety of tastes with citrus on the inside and llamas on the outside: one for eating, the other for petting.

The Trip
Take a wonderful journey back in time! Boyette's Grove is called a "citrus attraction," but I found it to be that and so much more. It started as a small fruit stand in the early '60s, and in many ways, it still has the feel of an old Florida roadside attraction.

What To See
This place is loaded with so many things rolled into one! First and foremost, it is a real citrus operation. Watch oranges and grapefruit roll down the processing chute and get sized and graded. Along with the citrus, the gift shop is full of fun stuff and Florida souvenirs. You'll also find a small aquarium inside and an ice cream shop offering 24 taste-tempting flavors. You can spend hours here.

Other Highlights
Don't forget to head out back where you'll find a nice little zoo, a walk-through aviary and a kids play area. I told you this place had a lot going on!

4355 Spring Lake Highway
Brooksville, FL 34601
(800) 780-2296
(352) 796-2289

Admission: *Grove and store free. Zoo admission $2.95 for adults, $1.95 for children 3-16, free for children 2 and under.*

Hours: *Groves open daily. Zoo open 10 a.m. to 5 p.m. in summer, 9 a.m. to 5 p.m. in winter. Closed Monday.*

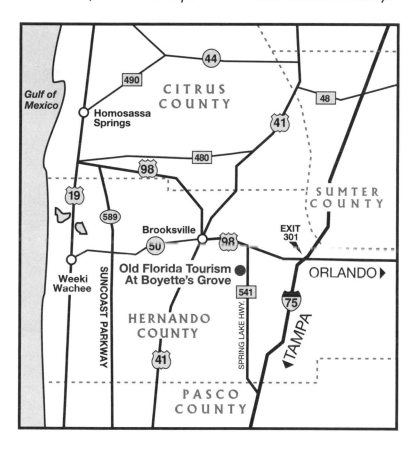

Directions

From Tampa, take Interstate 75 north to the U.S. 98/Brooksville exit (Exit #301). Turn left and go west to C.R. 541/Spring Lake Highway. Turn left and go south on C.R. 541. After about 1.5 miles, groves and retail store are at the top of a hill.

"EXPERIENCE AN OLD-TIME FLORIDA ATTRACTION."

Central Florida

Polk Museum Of Art
MORE THAN AN ART MUSEUM

Polk Museum Of Art

This beautiful building is filled with a celebration of art.

Polk Museum Of Art

The Trip
This "One Tank" takes you to Central Florida's premiere art museum. In addition to the breathtaking artwork, you'll also find films, live shows and classes for students of all ages.

What To See
You'll discover nine galleries as you explore this 37,000-square-foot facility. The museum has a permanent collection, but it also hosts about two dozen different shows a year. You can enjoy the work of professional artists as well as offerings from local students. Make sure you see the sculpture garden outside. The centerpiece is a beautiful wall of water that is a treat for both your eyes and your ears. When students visit, they are encouraged to close their eyes and imagine what the rushing water sounds like. On my visit, one youngster proclaimed, "It sounds like chicken frying!"

Other Highlights
You can enjoy hundreds of live shows and movies during the year in the Kent Harrison Auditorium. Don't forget to finish up your visit with a trip to the gallery gift shop where some very artistic, unique and fun stuff awaits.

800 E. PALMETTO STREET LAKELAND, FL 33801 (863) 688-7743

Central Florida

Admission: $3 for adults, $2 for students with ID, children under 5 free. $10 for families. Free Saturday until noon.

Hours: Tuesday through Saturday, 10 a.m. to 5 p.m., 1 p.m. to 5 p.m. Sunday. Closed Monday and most major holidays.

www.polkmuseumofart.org

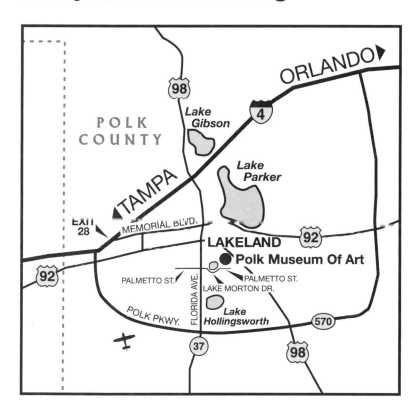

Directions

From Tampa, take Interstate 4 east to Memorial Boulevard (Exit #28). Take Memorial Boulevard into Lakeland. (It will turn into U.S. 92.) Turn right and go south on Florida Avenue. Then turn left on East Palmetto Street, which briefly becomes Lake Morton Drive around a lake. Follow to the library (you can park behind the building).

"A NICE WAY TO SPEND PART OF A RAINY DAY – OR A SUNNY ONE."

Retired Horse Farm Experience

WHERE HORSES GO TO BE LOVED

Central Florida

Retirement Home For Horses

A safe and happy home for horses.

The Trip

The Retirement Home for Horses is one of my favorite "One Tank Trips," even though you can only visit on Saturdays. The price of admission is two carrots, but I suggest you bring a whole bunch!

What To See

This is a special place dedicated to rescuing and caring for old, abused and unwanted horses. For more than 20 years, Peter and Mary Gregory have called this place home. So, too, have hundreds of horses. More than 125 of them currently share these 245 acres. All horses are promised two things: they will never be worked or ridden again and this will be their home where they will live out their lives. With every horse comes a story. Some horses are retired from police departments, while others used to pull carriages in crowded cities. Many of these animals are arthritic, some are blind, but all are well cared for by the staff and volunteers.

Other Highlights

If you want to experience the horses up close and personal, volunteers 18 and older are invited to groom a horse on Thursdays and Saturdays. There is also a picnic area and five hiking trails. You might be surprised to see that the farm is home to a lot of friendly dogs. I couldn't help but laugh as I watched them compete with the horses for my attention. Also ask about their "adopt-a-horse" program.

Retirement Home For Horses At Mill Creek Farm
20307 NW County Road 235-A
Alachua, FL 32616
(386) 462-1001

Admission: *Two carrots. Donations accepted.*

Hours: *Open Saturday, 11 a.m. to 3 p.m.*

www.millcreekfarm.org

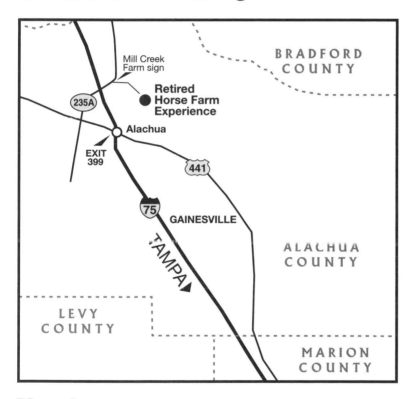

Directions

From Tampa, take Interstate 75 north. Go to Alachua/ High Springs/U.S. 441 exit (Exit #399). Turn left and go west on U.S. 441. Continue to C.R. 235-A. Turn right and go north. After about two miles, go over a bridge. Right after the bridge, on the right, is a white gravel and dirt driveway. Turn right into Mill Creek Farm. At the end of the driveway, continue through the gate and you'll see cars parked on the right.

"With Every Horse Comes A Story."

Central Florida

Rock & Roll Museum
WHERE THE MUSIC COMES ALIVE

The ideal guitar for surf music.

Hard Rock

Walk along the corridor of rock & roll memorabilia.

Hard Rock

The Trip
Here's a chance to take a peek inside the "vault" and enjoy its wealth of treasures. You'll find a huge array of rock & roll memorabilia while listening to your favorite tunes.

What To See
This is a place where rock & roll is still king. There are posters and records on display everywhere, along with a whole lot of rockin' memorabilia. It's a total immersion tour. You're surrounded by rock & roll history. You can spend hours just reading about each item. There are guides around as well, dressed up in '50s and '60s clothing. Be sure to explore the numerous rooms and galleries spread out over the 17,000 square feet of displays and interactive exhibits. There are nearly 1,000 artifacts in all. Some of my favorites include Jimmy Page's double-neck Gibson guitar, and a crown and red cape once worn by the "Godfather of Soul," James Brown. Don't miss the display of the famous leather pants worn by the Doors' lead singer, Jim Morrison.

Other Highlights
It's okay to question the guides and costumed actors. In fact, they welcome it. The gift shop is a must stop. It's full of souvenirs and rock & roll-themed items.

Hard Rock Vault
8437 International Drive
Orlando, FL 32819
(407) 599-7625

Admission: *$14.95 for adults, $8.95 for children 6-12, children under 6 free.*

Hours: *Open daily, 9 a.m. to midnight. Last ticket sold at 10 p.m.*

www.hardrock.com/vault

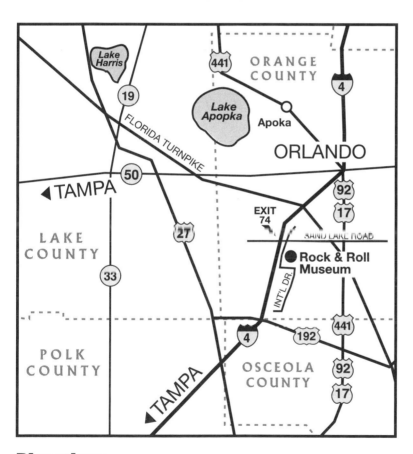

Directions

From Tampa, take Interstate 4 east to Sand Lake Road/ International Drive (Exit #74). Turn right and go east. Take a right on International Drive. Building is ahead on the left at entrance to Mercado shopping center.

" GIVE ME THAT OLD TIME ROCK & ROLL."

Big Cat Rescue
A WELL-DESERVED SAFE HAVEN

Hillsborough County – West Central Florida

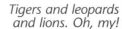
Tigers and leopards and lions. Oh, my!

Jamie Veronica

Jamie Veronica

The Trip

I was amazed to learn that I could come nose-to-nose with wildlife a stone's throw from a major mall in Citrus Park. More than 170 exotic cats call this place home.

What To See

Lions, tigers, leopards, cougars and more. Each has a special story. Many of these big cats came from circuses where they got too old to perform and were about to be destroyed. Others were former "pets" of people who didn't realize what they were getting into. Ask to see Nikita who is also called "Nicky." She is a beautiful young lioness who was found in the basement of a drug dealer in Nashville, Tenn. She and the others are now safe and healthy, cared for and loved. Be sure to bring your camera along on the 90 minute tour. Participants need to be at least 10 years old. A special Saturday tour is available for the younger set.

Other Highlights

There are numerous volunteer programs as well as special animal interaction activities. You can even spend the night with the big cats! Ask about this on your visit or check the web site.

12802 EASY STREET
TAMPA, FL 33625
(813) 920-4130

Admission: *$20 per person 10 or older. Children 10 and under allowed only during special 9 a.m. Saturday tour.*

Hours: *Monday through Friday, tours at 9 a.m. and 3 p.m.; Saturday, tours at 9:30 a.m., 11:30 a.m. and 1:30 p.m. Closed Sunday. Night tour on last Friday of each month at 8 p.m.*

www.bigcatrescue.org

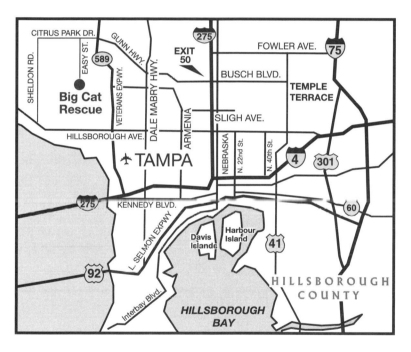

Directions

From Tampa, take Interstate 275 north to Busch Boulevard (Exit # 50). Turn left and go west. Busch Boulevard becomes Gunn Highway. Pass under green overpass (Veterans Expressway). Look for McDonald's on left. Dirt road next to McDonald's is Easy Street. You have to drive past McDonald's and turn around. There is no left turn available opposite Easy Street. Turn and follow road about half a mile to the end.

"A REFUGE FOR WILD REFUGEES."

Camp Bayou

WHERE ANCIENT HISTORY COMES ALIVE

Hillsborough County – West Central Florida

Camp Bayou Outdoor Learning Center

Study the fossils that fill the area.

Camp Bayou Outdoor Learning Center

Canoe along the serene waters at your own pace.

The Trip

Ready for a fun trip back in time? This pristine 200-acre outdoor camp sits on the banks of the Little Manatee River and it has some ancient history to share with visitors.

What To See

They call this place an environmental and hands-on learning center. I call it fun! Be sure to take time to enjoy the many peaceful and beautiful nature trails here. But also be sure to make time for the paleo preserve, which has a wide range of fossils from Florida and all over the world. Children particularly enjoy getting up close and in touch with a giant pig skull and the bones of a saber tooth tiger. Kids are even invited to dig in an outdoor pit that has been seeded with fossils. You'll find bits of ancient turtle shells, bones and even sharks' teeth. Whatever you find, you get to keep.

Other Highlights

School groups are welcome here for scheduled field trips. Bring a picnic lunch and dine "riverside." You can also rent a canoe for a leisurely paddle.

CAMP BAYOU
OUTDOOR LEARNING CENTER
4202 24TH STREET SE
RUSKIN, FL 33570
(813) 641-8545

TRIP
16

Admission: *Free*

Hours: *Open Thursday through Saturday, 10 a.m. to 3 p.m.; closed Sunday through Wednesday.*

www.campbayou.org

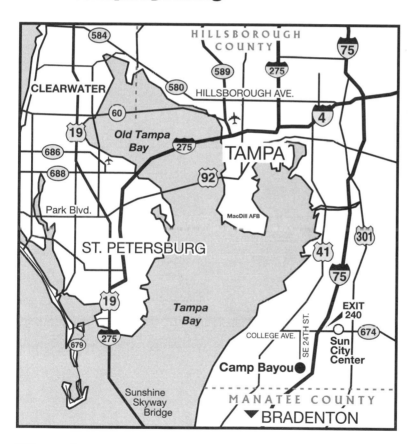

Directions
From Tampa, take Interstate 75 south to Exit #240. Turn right and go west on S.R. 674 (College Avenue) about 1 mile to 24th Street SE. Turn left and go south 3 miles. Road ends in park. Take left at second set of gates.

"LEARNING THE FUN WAY."

DolphinQuest Ecotour

ENJOYING OUR NEIGHBORHOOD DOLPHINS

Hillsborough County – West Central Florida

The Florida Aquarium

Tampa Bay dolphins like to show off by leaping and splashing.

The Florida Aquarium

On the lookout for dolphins.

The Trip

There's a dolphin or two waiting to spend some "quality time" with you. Hop aboard the Florida Aquarium's 64-foot Caribbean catamaran "The Bay Spirit" and you're good to go!

What To See

A great many dolphins call the waters of Tampa Bay home, so chances are very good you'll get to meet up with more than a few of them on this delightful cruise. Expect to see them when you enter the mouth of the Alafia River. You'll also spend some time off of the Alafia bird sanctuary, a beautiful little island that thousands of birds, more than 20 species, call home. The crew narrates the tour, sharing facts about dolphins and the need to protect them. In fact, the crew makes this trip so often, they get to know some dolphins by sight. For example, there's Fin, so named because he doesn't have one. Be sure to bring a camera.

Other Highlights

Of course the boat ride alone is worth the price. But if you'd like to combine your boat ride with a trip to the Aquarium, combination tickets are available.

THE FLORIDA AQUARIUM
701 CHANNELSIDE DRIVE
TAMPA, FL 33602
(813) 273-4000

Admission: *$18.95 for adults; $17.95 for seniors (60+); $13.95 for children 3-11; free for children 2 and under. Reservations not accepted.*

Tour Hours: *Tour hours vary by season. Please call ahead for tour times.*

www.flaquarium.org

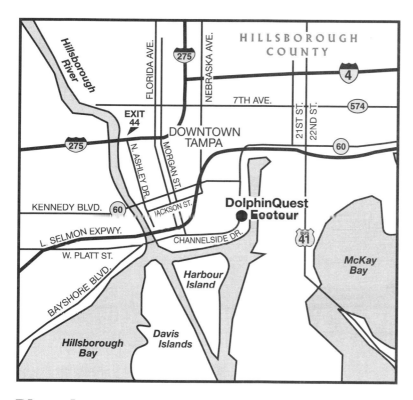

Directions

From Tampa, take Interstate 275 north to North Ashley Drive (Exit #44). Head south on Ashley to Jackson Street. Turn left at Jackson and head to Morgan Street. Turn right on Morgan to Channelside Drive. Turn left and follow Channelside and the Aquarium will be ahead on your right. Signs will direct you to parking.

"A COOL PLACE TO COOL OFF."

TRIP 18

Hillsborough River Canoe Escape
PADDLING AT YOUR OWN PACE

Tampa Bay Convention & Visitors Bureau

Take a paddle in hand and smoothly glide along these pristine waters.

Tampa Bay Convention & Visitors Bureau

Birds abound along the shores of the Hillsborough River, just a few miles from metropolitan Tampa.

The Trip
This "One Tank" getaway is just a short drive from Downtown Tampa, yet you would never know it once you're out on the beautiful Hillsborough River. Surrounded by the sights and sounds of nature, it will feel as if you've been transported to another time.

What To See
Treat yourself to a canoe or kayak trip down this beautiful, old river. You don't have to be an expert to take a paddle in hand and smoothly glide along these pristine waters. There are plenty of Florida's natural splendors to behold. Don't be surprised if you pass by some snoozing alligators. You'll also get the chance to see ibis, turkeys, deer and even the occasional wild hog. The friendly folks at the Canoe Escape take care of everything. They drop you off upstream and when you're finished, they're there to pick you up and take you back to your car.

Other Highlights
If you're looking for something a little different, try the moonlight canoe trips. All you need is a flashlight since everything else is provided. There's nothing quite like the thrill of shining that light out into the darkness and spotting some bright eyes staring back at you from the shore!

9335 E. Fowler Avenue
Thonotosassa, FL 33592
(813) 986-2067

Admission: *Rental rates vary according to size of canoe and length of trip. Call for prices.*

Hours: *Open Monday through Friday, 9 a.m. to 5 p.m., Saturday and Sunday, 8 a.m. to 5 p.m. Last launch, 2 p.m.*

www.canoeescape.com

Directions

From Tampa, take Interstate 275 north to I-4. Take I-4 east to I-75 north (Exit #9). On I-75, take first exit, Fowler Avenue (Exit #265). Turn right and go east. Canoe Escape is the on right after about one-half mile, across the street from Big Top Flea Market.

"Enjoy the tranquility of this beautiful spot."

In The Breeze Horse Camp

HORSE COUNTRY OF CARROLLWOOD

Hillsborough County – West Central Florida

A place for a horse of course, of course.

The Trip

"Howdy partner. New in town?" You'll get right into the swing of things when you arrive at this horse camp just a stone's throw from downtown Tampa.

What To See

You'll find more than one hundred horses on this 300 acre ranch and more than 80 of them will be more than happy to take you for a ride. If you're not experienced, ask for Dream. He's the horse anyone can ride. Head on out for a one hour adventure. If you like, you can also arrange for a private riding lesson. Be sure to stop by the petting zoo. Llamas, goats, emus, dogs, chickens, ducks and heaven knows what else eagerly await your arrival!

Other Highlights

How about a fun, old fashioned hay ride? They're easy to schedule. Fridays and Saturdays in October, come on out for the nighttime, very scary Halloween hayride. In December the weekend hay rides celebrate the holiday season.

7514 GARDNER ROAD
TAMPA, FL 33625
(813) 264-1919

Admission: *Free. Horseback riding $25 for first hour, $20 for each additional hour.*

Hours: *Open 8 a.m. to 5 p.m. seven days a week, 365 days a year.*

www.inthebreezeranch.com

Directions

From Tampa, take Veterans Expressway north to Linebaugh Avenue (Exit #7). Go west on Linebaugh to Sheldon Road. Turn right and go north on Sheldon Road. The first street on the right is Gardner Road. Turn right and go east on Gardner to where road forks. Take left fork and follow signs. Road deadends at the camp.

"A SWELL PLACE TO HORSE AROUND."

Jibac Gallery
A CELEBRATION OF CULTURE

Hillsborough County – West Central Florida

Jibac Gallery

Jibac Gallery

One man's dream is displayed in the framed artworks on the gallery walls. Paintings, culture and crafts abound.

The Trip

How would you like to gaze upon the treasures of Africa without boarding a plane for Kenya or Cameroon? All you need to do is take a drive to the University Mall and pay Joel Ilesan's Jibac Gallery a visit. This place is a dream come true for a man building bridges between Africa and the people of Tampa Bay.

What To See

This is a place filled with very affordable paintings, sculptures and native crafts from more than twenty countries, including Joel's homeland of Nigeria. Here you'll find offerings from Ghana, Senegal, Gambia and South Africa to name just a few. While the paintings are spectacular, I found myself drawn to the ebony wood carvings that capture ancient traditions and modern cultures. The detail is unbelievable. If you like to wear your art, make sure you look through the fabulous dashikis. These beautiful garments are handmade by Joel's sister.

Other Highlights

This is one destination where you don't have to worry about parking! Believe me, the mall's parking lot has plenty of room for you. The gallery also boasts a fine framing shop.

University Mall
2200 E. Fowler Avenue
Tampa, FL 33612
(866) 542-2227
(813) 975-1094

Admission: Free

Hours: 10 a.m. to 9 p.m. Monday through Saturday, noon to 6 p.m. Sunday. Closed Thanksgiving, Christmas and New Year's Day.

www.jibacgallery.com

Directions
From Tampa, take Interstate 275 north to Fowler Avenue (Exit #51). Turn right and go east on Fowler Avenue. Mall will be one mile ahead on the left.

"OUT OF AFRICA."

Little Manatee Canoe Outpost

A THEME PARK ALTERNATIVE

Hillsborough County – West Central Florida

A double-bladed paddle and sunglasses—that's just about all you need to enjoy a jaunt along the Little Manatee River.

Little Manatee River Canoe Outpost

The Trip

When you need a break from Florida's heat, head for the Little Manatee River. Even in August, the water temperature is a rejuvenating 76 degrees!

What To See

The Little Manatee Canoe Outpost is only 30 minutes south of either Tampa or St. Petersburg. This is a special river because it's designated an "Outstanding Florida Waterway." That means it has the highest level of water quality in the state. Don't worry about overdoing it. A steady three-mile-an-hour current makes for easy paddling. The river is mostly shallow and has a beautiful white, sandy bottom. The trip originates in a hardwood forest but soon you'll find yourself in a tropical paradise complete with giant ferns and palm trees. Keep an eye out for alligators, turtles and otters. If you're lucky, you might even spot an eagle overhead. You can spend an hour or the whole day exploring this "off the beaten path" destination.

Other Highlights

There's more than boating available at this outpost. You'll find picnic pavilions, rest rooms, a hiking trail and nature walks all along the river.

18001 U.S. Hwy. 301 S.
Wimauma, FL 33598
(813) 634-2228

Admission: *Rates vary according to length of trip and type of boat. Rates start at $23. Reservations suggested.*

Hours: *Open daily, 9 a.m. to 5 p.m. Closed Wednesday. Open Christmas and Thanksgiving by appointment only.*

www.canoeingfun.com
www.canoeoutpost.com/ LittleManatee.html

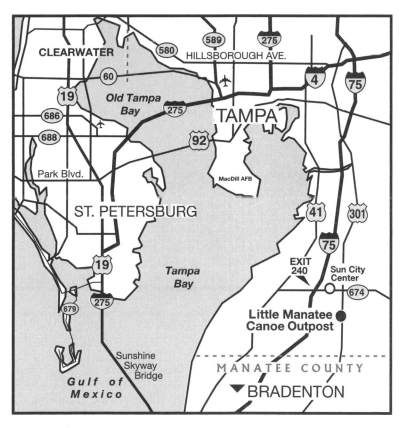

Directions

From Tampa, take Interstate 75 south to S.R. 674/Sun City Center Boulevard (Exit #240). Turn left and go east to U.S. 301. Then turn right and go south on U.S. 301 for about three miles.

"A Cool And Beautiful Part Of Florida."

Lowry Park Zoo River Odyssey Ecotour

UP A LAZY RIVER...

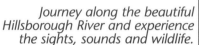

Journey along the beautiful Hillsborough River and experience the sights, sounds and wildlife.

Lowry Park Zoo

Lowry Park Zoo

The Trip

Take a relaxing and educational journey up the Hillsborough River. During the trip, you'll learn about plants, animals and history along this lovely stretch of waterway.

What To See

The adventure starts at the entrance to the Lowry Park Zoo. After you buy your tickets, you'll take a short tram ride to the riverbank. From there, you'll board the catamaran "Sirenia" and your river odyssey begins. This hour-long narrated voyage covers about two miles of the river. Be sure to keep an eye out for native birds, turtles and dozens of other animals. You might be lucky enough to catch a glimpse of one of Florida's gentle giants, a manatee. Be sure to say "thanks" to Ol' Man River for a great afternoon.

Other Highlights

If you buy a combo ticket to the Zoo and the River Odyssey Ecotour, you'll get $2 off the total purchase price. The Lowry Park Zoo itself is a great destination. Be sure to check out the Manatee Encounter when you visit.

1101 W. SLIGH AVENUE
TAMPA, FL 33604
(813) 935-8552

Admission: *Ecotour fees are $10 for adults, $9 for seniors (50+) and $7 for children 3-11. Admission to zoo is $11.50 for adults, $10.50 for seniors (50+) and $7.95 for children 3-11. Children 2 and under, free.*

Ecotour Hours: *Operates seven days a week at various times. Contact the zoo for daily running times. Closed Thanksgiving and Christmas.*

www.lowryparkzoo.com

Directions

From Tampa, take Interstate 275 north to the Sligh Avenue (Exit #48). Turn left and go west on Sligh. The zoo is at the corner of Sligh and North Boulevard. The Ecotour participants are shuttled from the zoo to the boat.

"BE SURE TO SAY 'THANKS' TO OL' MAN RIVER."

TRIP 23

Manatee Viewing Center
OH, MAN! OH, MAN! OH, MANATEES!

Hillsborough County – West Central Florida

There are more manatees here in the winter time than you can shake a camera at.

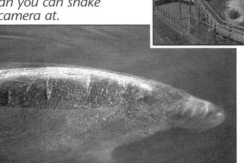

TECO Energy

The TECO Energy power plant pulls in hundreds of manatees seeking warm water.

TECO Energy

The Trip

This "One Tank Trip" is about cold weather, warm water and gentle giants! The Manatee Viewing Center at the TECO Big Bend Power Station is a great place for kids and grown-ups.

What To See

Winter is the best time of year to see the manatees here. Warm water flowing out of the power plant attracts these slow moving creatures in huge numbers. The power company built a viewing platform back in 1986, and it's been a big hit ever since. You'll get a great view of the manatees, including some moms with their newborns. If you watch carefully, you might see one of the babies come up for a breath of air. A few good tips: Wear polarized sunglasses to better see the manatees in the water. If you have binoculars, bring them!

Other Highlights

Be sure to allow extra time to take a stroll on the nature trail boardwalk. This takes you out into an unspoiled tidal area where you can see birds, fish and plant life. I also recommend visiting the Environmental Educational Building where you'll find a number of interesting exhibits. Round it all out with a trip to the gift shop. Even though some manatees are present year round, the viewing center is closed mid-April through mid-November.

TECO Big Bend Power Station
6990 Dickman Road
Apollo Beach, FL 33572
(813) 228-4289

Admission: *Free*

Hours: *Open Nov. 1 through mid-April, dawn to dusk.*

www.manatee-teco.com

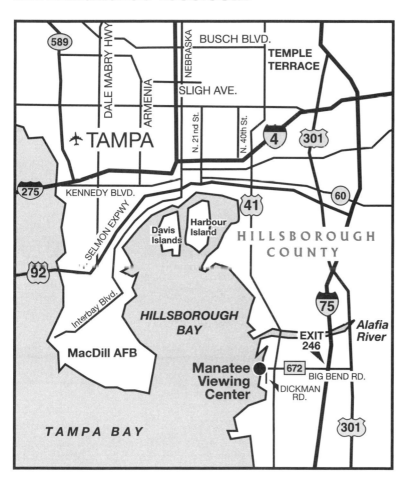

Directions

From Tampa, take Interstate 75 south to C.R. 672/Big Bend Road (Exit #246). Turn right and go west on Big Bend Road. Travel 2.5 miles west to the corner of Big Bend Road and Dickman Road. The center entrance is on the right.

"COLD WEATHER, WARM WATER AND GENTLE GIANTS!"

Old McMicky's Farm
A HANDS-ON FARM FOR KIDS

Kids of all ages get to be farmers for a day.

Old McMicky's Farm

Getting up close and personal with "Bessie."

Old McMicky's Farm

Old McMicky's Farm

You can snuggle up to a bunny.

The Trip

Tucked away in Odessa is an honest-to-goodness hands-on farm for kids and city boys like me. By the end of your trip you might be singing "Old McMicky had a farm, ee-ii-ee-ii-oo."

What To See

You can take a gander at a goose, milk a cow or ride a pony. If you don't want to ride a pony, how about a mule? You will also want to spend some time with the farm's goats and say "Hi" to the ducks and bunnies, too. Make time to visit Bonnie, the pig, all 450 pounds of her. If you want some real exercise, you can even chase a chicken or two.

Other Highlights

All visitors get a guided tour through the farm that's very educational. In addition to the animals, there is an amazing treehouse that your kids will love. Don't miss the old-fashioned hay rides.

19215 Crescent Road
Odessa, FL 33556
(813) 920-1948

Admission: *General admission, $8 plus tax (cash only); free for children under 2. Closed Easter, Thanksgiving, Christmas and New Year's Day. Guests are urged to call ahead.*

Hours: *Open Monday through Saturday. First tour at 9:30 a.m.; last tour at 1:45 p.m. Closed Sunday.*

www.oldmcmickysfarm.com

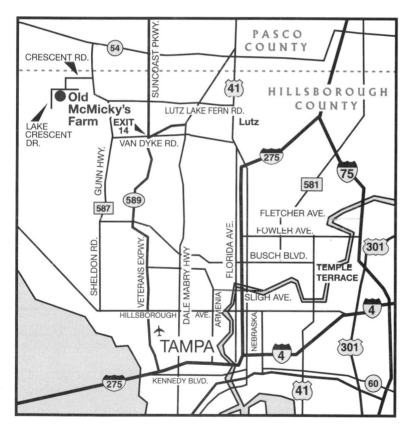

Directions

From Tampa, take Veterans Expressway to Van Dyke Road (Exit #14). Turn left and go west to Gunn Highway. Turn right on go north on Gunn to Crescent Road. Turn left on Crescent Road and follow to Camp Keystone parking area.

"YOU CAN EVEN CHASE A CHICKEN OR TWO."

Plant City Historic Train Tours

RIDING THE RAILS INTO HISTORY

Hillsborough County – West Central Florida

All aboard for a day of training!

Plant City Chamber Of Commerce

Plant City Chamber Of Commerce

The Trip

When it comes to trains, this place is right on track! The Union Station Historic District Train Depot and Museum is a must for train buffs of all ages.

What To See

The depot is full of interesting artifacts. There is an authentic ticket office with traditional green benches in the waiting room. You'll also find official railroad "dining car" china on display in cabinets. I enjoyed looking at all the vintage signs and billboards. It made me feel like I was looking through a window into the past. You might be surprised to find that modern day trains still use this station. We were lucky enough to see a few CSX trains thunder by during our visit.

Other Highlights

Just a few blocks away, you can also visit a collection of smaller trains preserved by the H.B. Plant Railroad Historical Society. It's located in the 1914 Plant City High School Community Center, on Collins Street. As far as I'm concerned, your visit's not complete until you drop by the Whistle Stop Café and enjoy one of their famous five cent "Cherry Smash" sodas.

102 N. PALMER STREET
PLANT CITY, FL 33566
(813) 719-6989

Admission: Free

Hours: Open Thursday through Saturday, 10 a.m. to 4 p.m. Closed Sunday through Wednesday and major holidays.

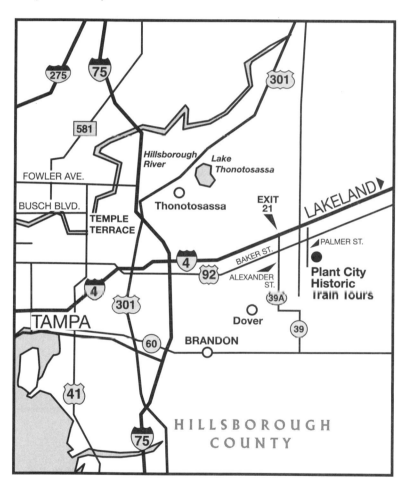

Directions

From Tampa, take Interstate 4 east to Alexander Street (Exit #21). Turn right and go south to Baker Street/U.S. 92. Turn left and go east about one mile to Palmer Street. Turn right. The station and depot are in the middle of Old Historic Plant City, about two blocks ahead on the left.

"A 'ONE TANK TRIP' THAT'S RIGHT ON TRACK."

S.S. American Victory
A "CRUISE" BACK IN TIME

Hillsborough County – West Central Florida

S.S. American Victory Mariners Memorial & Museum Ship

Volunteers spent thousands of hours renovating and reconditioning the American Victory so it could sail once again.

The Trip
Here's a chance to take a "cruise" back in time without ever setting sail. This proud ship saw duty during World War II, the Korean War and the Vietnam War. You can easily find it docked next to the Florida Aquarium near downtown Tampa.

What To See
The former Merchant Marine vessel has called Tampa home since 1999. The whole crew is proud of the work they did to restore the "Victory" to sailing condition. It is one of the few ships of its kind still open to the public. Visitors enter through the "#3 Cargo Hold." Self-guided tours include the deckhouse, living spaces, the engine room and the weather deck. Volunteers are usually on hand to answer questions.

Other Highlights
A few times a year, the S.S. American Victory sets sail and you can take part! The six to eight hour cruise goes all the way out to the Sunshine Skyway Bridge before heading back to port. Guests are treated to a gourmet meal, a live band and the crew decked out in authentic uniforms. Call for more information about the next voyage.

705 CHANNELSIDE DRIVE
BERTH #271
TAMPA, FL 33602
(813) 228-8766

Admission: *$8 for adults (13 and older), $7 for seniors (50+), $3 for children 3-12, free for children under 3.*

Hours: *Monday through Saturday, 10 a.m. to 4 p.m.; Sunday, noon to 5 p.m.*

www.americanvictory.com

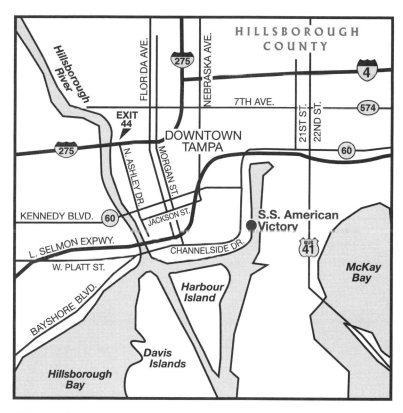

Directions

From Tampa, take Interstate 275 north to North Ashley Drive (Exit #44). Head south on Ashley to Jackson Street. Turn left at Jackson and head to Morgan Street. Turn right on Morgan to Channelside Drive. Turn left and follow Channelside. The Aquarium will be ahead on your right. Signs will direct you to parking.The ship is located behind the Aquarium.

Hillsborough County – West Central Florida

"AN AMERICAN BEAUTY."

Sharks!
DIVE WITH THE SHARKS
AT THE FLORIDA AQUARIUM

Hillsborough County – West Central Florida

Up close and personal with sharks at the Florida Aquarium.

The Florida Aquarium

The Trip

This is a rarity—a "One Tank" in a tank. The Florida Aquarium, the gem along Tampa's Channelside waterfront, offers the brave and curious a chance to get into the water with a shark or two. Don't worry, it's quite safe but you must be a certified diver.

What To See

Before you descend into the shark tank, it's off to a classroom for some instruction where you'll learn all about your upcoming dive. You'll spend time talking about the real stars of this show, the sharks, and the many misconceptions about these amazing and important animals. Once you "graduate," your divemaster will accompany you into the tank. The experience is more amazing than I could ever imagine: zebra sharks, sand tiger sharks, black tip and white tip reef sharks, nurse sharks and even a very friendly green sea turtle are all waiting to greet you.

Other Highlights

In addition to your memories and newly acquired shark tales, divers also get a certificate and a complimentary T-shirt that proclaims that you swam with the sharks! Don't forget to explore the rest of the Florida Aquarium, since you're right there.

THE FLORIDA AQUARIUM
701 CHANNELSIDE DRIVE
TAMPA, FL 33602
(813) 273-4000

Admission: *$150 for 90-minute program and 30-minute dive. Includes admission to the aquarium.*

Hours: *Dives vary by season. Please call ahead for dive times. Reservations required.*

www.flaquarium.com

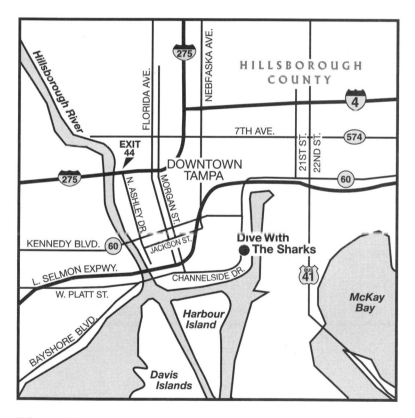

Directions

From Tampa, take Interstate 275 north to North Ashley Drive (Exit #44). Head south on Ashley to Jackson Street. Turn left at Jackson and head to Morgan Street. Turn right on Morgan to Channelside Drive. Follow Channelside and the Aquarium will be ahead on your right. Signs will direct you to parking.

"A 'ONE TANK' IN A TANK."

Tampa Police Museum
A Look At Law Enforcement Now And Then

The department's first helicopter is on display.

Early police departments are remembered in photos.

Tampa Police Museum

Hillsborough County – West Central Florida

The Trip
This museum pays tribute to the history of Tampa's police department and to those police men and women who have fallen in the line of duty. It sits right downtown, so don't pass it by.

What To See
There are many old photos of early police officers, including a snapshot of the entire 1921 police department. There are other police items as well, including a genuine Thompson submachine gun taken from a Tampa gangster, known as "The Terrible Toohy." You can also see lots of police badges and patches from across the country. There's a golf cart converted into a police cart that was once used to patrol Ybor City, and even the department's first helicopter.

Other Highlights
At the museum's entrance stands a memorial to those who have given their lives in the line of duty. The museum gift shop has lots of souvenirs for sale including photos, shirts, pins, ball caps, T-shirts, key chains, jewelry, coffee mugs, figurines and more. All donations and purchases go toward the Gold Shield Fund, which supports widows and orphans of fallen police officers.

411 N. FRANKLIN STREET
2ND FLOOR
TAMPA, FL 33602
(813) 276-3258

Admission: *Free. Donations Accepted.*

Hours: *Monday through Friday, 10 a.m. to 3 p.m. Closed Saturday, Sunday and major holidays.*

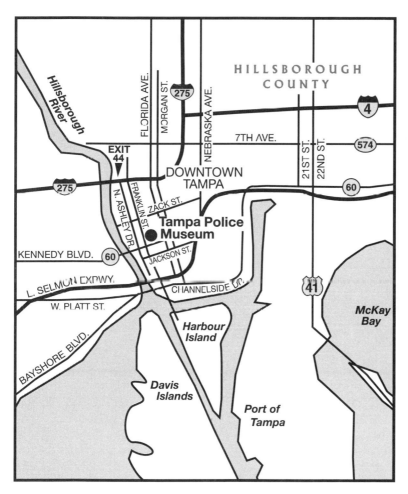

Directions

From Tampa, take Interstate 275 north to North Ashley Drive (Exit #44). Head south on Ashley, then turn left onto East Zack Street. Park near the corner of Zack and Franklin Streets (no cars are permitted on Franklin Street).

"A VERY INTERESTING LOOK AT THE WORLD OF LAW ENFORCEMENT."

Ybor City Walking Tour
LEARNING HISTORY AND HERITAGE

Hillsborough County – West Central Florida

Discover how Ybor City looks today.

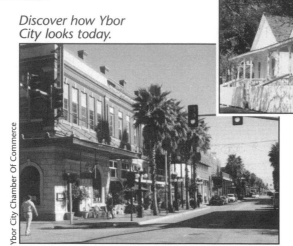

Ybor City Chamber Of Commerce

Ybor City Chamber Of Commerce

Part of the walking tour includes seeing the little houses or "casitas" that once were homes to Tampa's cigar makers.

The Trip

Ybor City isn't just a place for nighttime partying. There's plenty to do in the daytime as well. The Saturday morning guided walking tour gives visitors a ground-level view of this Latin quarter of Tampa and its rich history. It begins at the Ybor City State Museum. Before you begin your walk, spend some time inside the museum, enjoying the old photographs and memorabilia.

What To See

The tour begins at the museum's lush garden, then continues to beautiful Centennial Park and on to Ybor's "Main Street," 7th Avenue. Storefront after storefront, block after block, historic stories are found. The tour naturally includes the Ybor City Cigar Museum. Here visitors can see photos of the early cigar-making industry, as well as the rich artwork that adorned cigar boxes over the years gone by. You'll be able to learn about the history of the cigar industry so key to the growth of the Tampa Bay area. Be sure to notice the small cottages, called "casitas," built by Vincente Martinez Ybor for his cigar workers. The brick-lined streets, and especially 7th Avenue, are lined with cafés, restaurants and bars as well as a number of other small shops, including antique stores. Many have been restored to their early glory.

Other Highlights

If possible, put the Columbia Restaurant at the end of your tour. This family-owned restaurant is the oldest in Florida, more than a century old. There are always authentic Cuban and Spanish dishes on the menu—and flamenco dancing six nights a week!

Ybor City State Museum
1818 9th Avenue
Ybor City, FL 33605
(813) 247-6323

Admission: *State museum admission is $3 per person; free for children 5 and under. Tours are offered on Saturday for $6, which includes admission to the museum. Tour takes about 60 minutes. Longer tours are available by appointment on Tuesday, Wednesday or Thursday for $12.*

Hours: *State museum is open 9 a.m. to 5 p.m. daily except major holidays. Tour starts at 10:30 a.m. Saturday.*

www.ybor.org

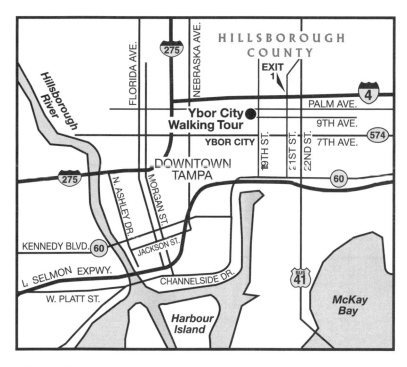

Directions
From Tampa, take Interstate 275 north to I-4. Go east on I-4 to Exit #1 (21st/22nd Street). Turn right and go south on 21st Street to Palm Avenue. Go right on Palm to 19th Street. Turn left. Museum is on 9th Avenue between 18th and 19th streets.

"IN THE FOOTSTEPS OF HISTORY."

Caladesi Island State Park
A VERY POPULAR ISLAND IN THE SUN

Pinellas County – West Central Florida

Caladesi Island State Park

Paddling along the shore at Caladesi Island.

Caladesi Island State Park

Lots of people like to visit the island for some serene sun and sand.

The Trip
There are beaches and then there's the beach at Caladesi Island. Year in and year out it's voted one of the very best beaches in America. But first you have to get there. Ferryboats leave every half hour year-round from Honeymoon Island.

What To See
Number one on our list of what to see is the magnificent beach with its fine white sand. You can stay on the island for up to four hours before your return trip. Hit the Gulf for a swim if you like or just find a beach chair and get real busy doing nothing. Later, try your hand at fishing or shell hunting. It's all up to you.

Other Highlights
Take a stroll along the three miles of nature trails. Stop by Café Caladesi for a very tasty experience. Rent a kayak and paddle out on a trail through the mangroves. For boat owners, the 108-slip marina is available for overnight stays for up to two weeks.

FERRY LEAVES FROM HONEYMOON ISLAND
ONE CAUSEWAY BLVD., DUNEDIN, FL 34698
(727) 469-5918

Admission: *Cash only. Entrance fees to Honeymoon Island are $5 per car for up to eight people, or $1 for individual entrance. Ferry charge is $8 for adults, $4.50 for children 4-12, free for children under 4. Picnic pavilion rental fees are $32.10. Call ahead at least 2 weeks for pavilion reservation.*

Hours: *Ferry leaves daily on the hour from Honeymoon Island starting at 10 a.m. Last return from Caladesi Island is 4:30 p.m. (4 hour maximum stay on Caladesi Island.)*

www.floridastateparks.org/caladesiisland

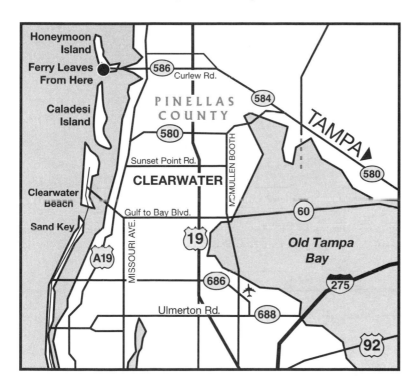

Directions
From Tampa, take Hillsborough Avenue/S.R. 580. Follow S.R. 580 west, continue straight at it becomes S.R. 584. After about two miles, road will split. Bear left at S.R. 586/Curlew Road. Follow Curlew west about six miles as it becomes Causeway Boulevard. Continue straight onto Honeymoon Island.

"AS GOOD
AS IT
GETS!"

Pinellas County – West Central Florida

TRIP 31

Capt. Bill's Yacht Cruises

A LEISURELY QUEST FOR SHELLS AND DOLPHINS

One goal for youngsters is a handful of personally found seashells.

Capt. Bill's Yacht Cruises

Capt. Bill's Yacht Cruises

Capt. Bill sails out of John's Pass for points nearby.

The Trip

Are you ready for a leisurely cruise to one of the Bay Area's most beautiful unspoiled beaches? Book a ticket on Capt. Bill's Yacht Cruises and you won't be disappointed.

What To See

Capt. Bill Macfarlane makes you feel right at home as soon as you step aboard his 50-foot yacht, the "Hakuna Matata." It's named after a popular song from the hit movie and musical "The Lion King." The "no worries" theme certainly is appropriate for Capt. Bill's sightseeing tours. This relaxing cruise is a perfect way to enjoy the best that Florida has to offer. Morning cruises stop off at picturesque Shell Island. In the afternoon, it's time to head out into the Gulf of Mexico in search of sea life. Dolphin sightings are just about guaranteed and the sunsets are breathtaking.

Other Highlights

Trips to Egmont Key are available by special charter. This tour includes a visit to a working lighthouse.

12765 Kingfish Drive
Treasure Island, FL 33708
(727) 319-2628

Admission: *Prices vary depending on tour.*

Hours: *Tours to Shell Island leave at 9 a.m. Dolphin watch tours leave at 1 p.m. and 3 p.m. Sunday sailings vary by season. Egmont Key trips by appointment.*

www.captainbillsboat.com

Directions

From Tampa, take Interstate 275 south to Exit #28 (Gandy Boulevard/S.R. 694). Turn right and go west to Seminole Boulevard/Alt. U.S. 19. Turn left on Seminole. As the road splits, take S.R. 666/Tom Stuart Causeway towards Madeira Beach. At Gulf Boulevard, turn left and go south. Cross over the John's Pass Bridge to Treasure Island. (John's Pass is directly across from the Gulf of Mexico.) Just over the bridge, turn first left.

"It's Not
About
Being
In A
Hurry."

Classic Autos At P.J.'s
A GREAT PLACE FOR A "RIDE" DOWN MEMORY LANE

TRIP 32

Pinellas County – West Central Florida

Classic autos are everywhere at the two showrooms.

Some cars come with an interesting history or even a celebrity or two.

The Trip

Talk about a classic! Talk about rooms full of them! This is where some very old and classy automobiles can be found. Come on in and have just a fine old time.

What To See

I flat out got lost in time here, and it's very easy to do. For those of us who grew up driving cars made in the 1950s and '60s, this place will seem like heaven-on-wheels. Indeed, you might find yourself humming tunes from a few years ago as you wander among the classics: Fords and Chevys and plenty of other brands, all gorgeously restored. Often, folks will stop by to relate stories of their "first rides" when they were young. Today's kids will drop in for a closer look at what cars were like when domestic makes ruled the highways "back in the good ol' days." Oh, by the way, they are also for sale.

Other Highlights

You might run into a famous face or two on your visit. Stars including Hulk Hogan, Kirstie Allie and John Travolta are on the celebrity customer list. There are two Clearwater locations. If you haven't seen enough at the first, head on over to the other one.

1370 CLEVELAND STREET
CLEARWATER, FL 33755
(800) 288-6386 OR (727) 461-4900

1751 GULF-TO-BAY BLVD.
CLEARWATER, FL 33755
(866) 820-4444 OR (727) 446-9999

Admission: *Free*

Hours: *Open Monday through Friday, 9 a.m. to 6 p.m.;
Saturday 9 a.m. to 5 p.m. Closed Sunday and major holidays.*

www.pjsautoworld.com

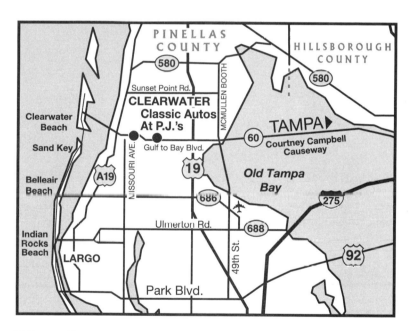

Directions

From Tampa, to the Gulf-to-Bay store, take Courtney Campbell Causeway/S.R. 60 west toward Clearwater. Continue on Courtney Campbell as it becomes Gulf-to-Bay Boulevard. Showroom is about 4 miles on the left. For the Cleveland Street store, continue past the Gulf-to-Bay store west to Cleveland Street. At Highland Avenue, the road continues and curves to the right. Take the curve to the right. Showroom is about one mile past Gulf-to-Bay, also on the right.

*"THIS PLACE
WILL
DEFINITELY
GET YOUR
MOTOR
RUNNIN'!"*

Classic Autos At P.J.'s

Dunedin Main Street
DELIGHTFULLY DIFFERENT

Pinellas County – West Central Florida

A walk through the quiet, small-town atmosphere of Dunedin is a shopping and dining experience you won't want to miss.

The Trip

A stroll along Dunedin's eight-block downtown is without question a "10." This quaint village-like atmosphere with Scottish flair offers an array of shops, restaurants and boutiques for all to enjoy! This delightful town was once home to the largest fleet of sailing vessels in Florida.

What To See

Be sure to visit the Dunedin Fish Market, which has quite a history. Inside, along with many catches of the day, you can "catch" a glimpse of the days gone by in photos of how the place looked a half-century ago. A shop called the Bohemian Pack Rat is another must stop. They call it "The Gallery of the Unusual," and there's no arguing with that. A few more paces down the brick-lined street, you'll find the old train station along with the Boxcar Restaurant. Afterwards, be sure to make a trip to the Dunedin Brewery, a true mom-and-pop operation. They offer daytime and evening tours and tastings.

Other Highlights

Main Street comes alive each February for a magical Mardi Gras celebration including parade floats, beads, food and fun. For those who enjoy biking and inline skating, the Pinellas Trail runs right through the center of Main Street.

DUNEDIN CHAMBER OF COMMERCE
301 MAIN STREET
DUNEDIN, FL 34698
(727) 733-3197

Admission: Free

Hours: Shops and stores open various hours, some depending on the seasons. Call ahead for specifics.

www.dunedin-fl.com
www.delightfuldunedin.com

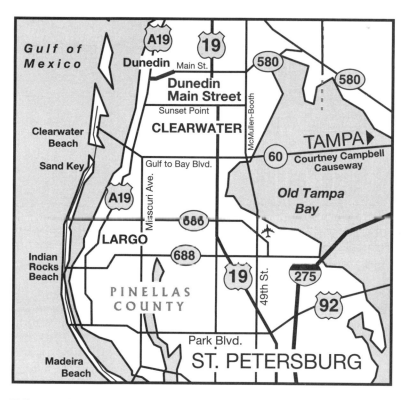

Directions

From Tampa, take Courtney Campbell Causeway/S.R. 60 west to U.S. 19. Turn right and go north on U.S. 19 to S.R. 580/Main Street. Turn left and go west. Follow signs to Dunedin. Main Street runs from Edgewater Drive (waterfront) to Milwaukee. There are also shops and restaurants along Douglas Avenue.

"A UNIQUE TOWN WITH A SCOTTISH FLAIR."

Florida Botanical Gardens

AN OASIS OF NATURAL BEAUTY

Pinellas County – West Central Florida

Florida Botanical Gardens

Florida Botanical Gardens

The gardens actually consist of several smaller themed gardens and green areas, including some ideal arbors for a wedding.

The Trip

A kaleidoscope of color awaits you at one of Tampa Bay's best-kept secrets. The Florida Botanical Gardens in Largo is a 150-acre oasis of themed gardens, rare plants and beautiful trees.

What To See

More than 10,000 plants are the stars of this show. You can find both Florida native and non-native ornamentals. We also discovered a collection of exotic and rare plants, including a Bismark Palm and a "national champion" silver buttonwood tree. One of the most popular spots is the Wedding Garden. This beautiful backdrop is actually made up of several smaller gardens and has been the site of hundreds of weddings. Master gardeners who volunteer their time and expertise maintain the entire Botanical Gardens.

Other Highlights

While at the gardens, you should also visit Heritage Village (profiled in our first "One Tank Trips" book). Heritage Village is a collection of more than 20 buildings that serve as a remarkable reminder of the state's rich heritage.

PINEWOOD CULTURAL PARK
12175 125TH STREET N.
LARGO, FL 33774
(727) 582-2200

Admission: *Free. Donations accepted.*

Hours: *Open daily, dawn to dusk. Welcome center open Monday through Saturday, 8 a.m. to 5 p.m.; Sunday, noon to 4 p.m.*

www.flbg.org

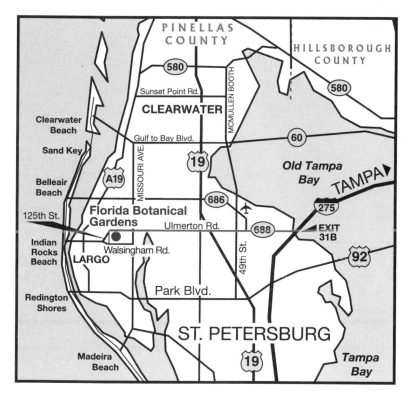

Directions

From Tampa, follow Interstate 275 south. Take Ulmerton Road/S.R. 688 (Exit #31B). Head west on Ulmerton toward the beaches for 10 miles. When Ulmerton bends to the south for a short distance, the next intersection is Walsingham Road. Turn left on Walsingham. Follow the signs to either the main entrance off of 125th Street, or the south entrance off Walsingham.

"ONE OF THE TAMPA BAY AREA'S BEST-KEPT SECRETS."

Gulf Beaches
Historical Museum

TAKE A HISTORICAL REVIEW
OF BEACH HISTORY

Pinellas County – West Central Florida

Inside, old photographs and artifacts are on display everywhere.

Gulf Beaches Historical Museum

The museum reflects the early architecture of the Gulf beaches.

The Trip

This Florida gem is located right in the heart of Pass-a-Grille, the historic village nestled at the south end of St. Pete Beach. The Museum is housed in the first church built on Pinellas County's barrier islands.

What To See

This museum gives you a true sense of what life was like along our beaches before World War II. You'll enjoy the photographs and artifacts from our past, long before condos and parking meters dotted the landscape. Among the photos, there are many old-time shots from John's Pass Bridge and Blind Pass. To see where early visitors stayed, look at the picture of Page's Pavilion, a bath and rooming house. On your drive to this museum, you'll pass by the "Pink Palace," the Don CeSar Resort which opened for business in 1928. The museum documents the amazing story of this great hotel.

Other Highlights

If you'd like a special tour for your group, the museum can easily accommodate you. Historical lectures, changing exhibits, fundraising events, and children's activities round out the Museum's calendar of events. The museum is a satellite facility of Pinellas County's Heritage Village. Check out the web site!

115 10TH AVENUE
ST. PETE BEACH, FL 33706
(727) 552-1610

Admission: Free. Donations Accepted.

Hours: Mid-May through mid-September, Friday and Saturday, 10 a.m. to 4 p.m.; Sunday, 1 p.m. to 4 p.m; mid-September through mid-May, Thursday through Saturday, 10 a.m. to 4 p.m.

www.co.pinellas.fl.us/bcc/
heritage/beach.htm

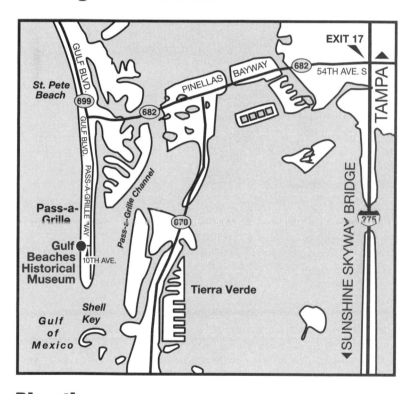

Directions

From Tampa, take Interstate 275 south to the Pinellas Bayway exit (Exit #17), just before reaching the Sunshine Skyway Bridge. There is a 50 cent toll on the Bayway. Take the Bayway west toward the Gulf of Mexico. It deadends into Gulf Boulevard. Turn left and go south. Continue straight on Gulf Boulevard as it becomes Pass-a-Grille Way. Turn right at 10th Avenue.

Pinellas County – West Central Florida

"BEACH LIFE
BACK IN
THE DAY."

Gulf Coast Museum Of Art

ᴀɴᴏᴛʜᴇʀ ʜɪᴅᴅᴇɴ ᴀʀᴛ ᴛʀᴇᴀsᴜʀᴇ

Pinellas County – West Central Florida

Gulf Coast Museum Of Art

Gulf Coast Museum Of Art

A lot of the artwork here requires more than just a quick look. Take some time to study the oils and sculptures.

The Trip

When it comes to well-kept secrets, this place has to be near the top of the list. At least, until now! If you're a modern art lover, plan on visiting this masterpiece in Largo.

What To See

I like to think of myself as a "child of the '60s." That's one reason why I am so attracted to this museum. The vast majority of the work here dates from 1960 and forward. The museum has nine galleries. Six of them house the permanent collection and the other three show new works of art. The artists represented are from Florida and the other southeastern states. The paintings are provocative, bold and beautiful. The museum also has a fabulous sculpture garden filled with unusual and compelling pieces. Before you go, make sure to check Paul Dellegatto's weather forecast so you can spend some leisurely time outside.

Other Highlights

The museum also has an auditorium that plays host to film and video screenings, lectures and art history classes. Be sure to call or check the museum's website for the latest programs.

PINEWOOD CULTURAL PARK
12211 WALSINGHAM ROAD
LARGO, FL 33778
(727) 518-6833

Admission: *$5 for adults, $4 for seniors (65+), $3 for students with ID, free for children 10 and under.*

Hours: *Open Tuesday through Saturday, 10 a.m. to 4 p.m; Sunday, noon to 4 p.m. Closed Monday and major holidays.*

www.gulfcoastmuseum.org

Directions
From Tampa, follow Interstate 275 south. Take Ulmerton Road/S.R. 688 (Exit #31B). Head west on Ulmerton toward the beaches for 10 miles. When Ulmerton bends to the south for a short distance, the next intersection is Walsingham Road. Turn left on Walsingham. Follow the signs to the main entrance.

"INSIDE YOU WILL FIND AN IMPRESSIVE COLLECTION."

H&R Trains
ON THE RIGHT TRACK FOR A MODEL RAILROADER'S PARADISE

Pinellas County – West Central Florida

All aboard! Some great trains, big and small, are on display. And even more are on sale to collectors and train enthusiasts.

The Trip
Gather up the kids and get on over to H&R Trains in Pinellas Park. This is one of the country's largest model train stores. It's wall to wall trains, tracks and a triumph of engineering ingenuity!

What To See
For three decades, this store has been a mecca for model railroaders. There are always trains in motion, scooting through towns, villages, mountains and valleys. The attention to detail is fantastic! People come from all over the country to shop for everything from locomotives to cabooses and everything in between. If they don't have it (which is a rare thing), they'll find it for you. One of the hottest items these days is the Hogwarts Express, the famous train that carries Harry Potter and all his fellow wizards. Of course, it's leaving from track 9 3/4. For you nostalgia buffs, check out the train bell from the last run on the old New York Central Railroad.

Other Highlights
There's a "Little Engineer's Club" for kids ranging in age from 3 to 7. They'll learn about real trains, make a craft project and get the opportunity to run the garden railroad. There's even a snack for the little ones. Best of all, it's FREE! Call for more details.

6901 U.S. 19 N.
PINELLAS PARK, FL 33781
(727) 526-4682

Admission: Free

Hours: Open Monday through Thursday, Saturday, 10 a.m. to 6 p.m.; Friday, 10 a.m. to 9 p.m.; Sunday, 11 a.m. to 5 p.m. Extended hours during the holiday season. Please call ahead.

www.hrtrains.com

Directions

From Tampa, take Interstate 275 south toward St. Petersburg. Take Gandy Boulevard/Park Boulevard (Exit #28) and head west. Stay on Park Boulevard until U.S. 19 (also called 34th Street). Turn left and go south on U.S. 19. Turn left at 64th Avenue North then left on Haines Road. H&R Trains will be at the end of the street on the right.

"WALL-TO-WALL TRAINS, TRACKS AND FUN."

K. Kringle's Christmas Shoppe

Ho! Ho! Ho! All Year Round

Christmas can always be found at this corner of St. Pete Beach.

The Hartigan family enjoys making holidays come alive every day of the year.

The Trip

There's no need to wait until December to get yourself in the Christmas spirit. Instead, head to St. Pete Beach for some 'rays and some wreaths!

What To See

Every time I go into K. Kringle's Christmas & Holiday Shoppe, I start thinking about Christmas memories from my childhood. Those good old days can be rediscovered with the holiday treasures that line the shelves and fill the floor in this unique establishment. There are Santas, angels and ornaments by the thousands. There are Christmas trees, silver bells, nutcrackers and elves. If it's about Christmas, you will find it here. You can even drop your Christmas wish list into Santa's mailbox.

Other Highlights

There are other holiday goodies, too. Peter Cottontail looks right at home in a shop full of reindeer. So do the Halloween costumes and Thanksgiving cornucopias!

400 75TH AVENUE
ST. PETE BEACH, FL 33706
(727) 367-1388

Admission: *Free*

Hours: *Monday through Saturday, 10 a.m. to 6 p.m; closed Sunday. Extended holiday hours: October 1 through December 23; Monday through Saturday, 10 a.m. to 8 p.m.; Sunday, noon to 5 p.m.*

www.kkringles.com

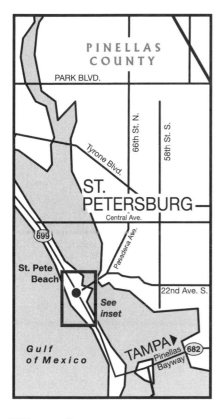

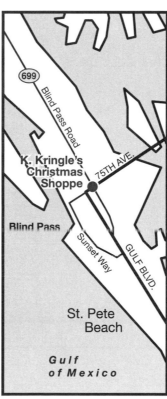

Directions

From Tampa, take Interstate 275 south to St. Petersburg. Continue to the Pinellas Bayway exit (Exit #17). Take Pinellas Bayway to Gulf Boulevard, turn right and go north. Continue to follow road to 75th Avenue (Corey Avenue). Turn right one block to Blind Pass Road. K. Kringle's is at intersection of Blind Pass Road and 75th Avenue

"LOTS AND LOTS OF SANTAS OF ALL SHAPES AND SIZES."

Leepa-Rattner Museum Of Art

WHERE ART FINDS EXPRESSION

Leepa-Rattner Museum Of Art

Inside, the spacious display areas invite contemplation.

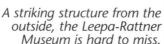

Leepa-Rattner Museum Of Art

A striking structure from the outside, the Leepa-Rattner Museum is hard to miss.

Pinellas County – West Central Florida

The Trip

If you want to immerse yourself in an array of magnificent 20th century art, take this "One Tank Trip" to the Tarpon Springs Campus of St. Petersburg College. You might opt to visit at night. The exterior design and lighting of this brand-new museum is stunning.

What To See

The museum is named for two of the giants of 20th century art. Abraham Rattner was known for his figurative expressions. His paintings are in museum collections around the world, including the Museum of Modern Art in New York City. Allen Leepa is Rattner's stepson and the driving force behind this museum. He is also well-known for his abstract expressionist paintings. Now, visitors can enjoy the works of both artists as well as the canvases and sketches by Rattner's friends, including Pablo Picasso, Marc Chagall, Georges Rouault and Henry Moore. Make sure you see the full-scale reproduction of Picasso's anti-war masterpiece, "Guernica."

Other Highlights

The 57,000-square-foot museum has numerous interactive displays that allow visitors to become "artists" as well. Also, the museum's auditorium plays host to film and video screenings, lectures and art history classes. Be sure to call or check the museum's web site for the latest programs.

600 KLOSTERMAN ROAD
PALM HARBOR, FL 34683
(727) 712-5762

Admission: *$5 for adults, $4 for seniors (62+). Free for children and students with ID. Sunday is free for everyone.*

Hours: *Tuesday, Wednesday, Friday, Saturday, 10 a.m. to 5 p.m.; Thursday, 10 a.m. to 9 p.m.; Sunday, 1 p.m. to 5 p.m. Closed Monday.*

www.spcollege.edu/museum

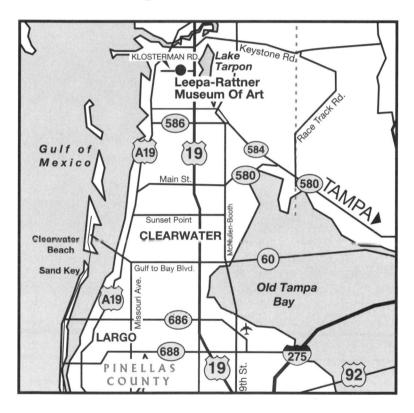

Directions
From Tampa, take Hillsborough Avenue/S.R. 580. Follow S.R. 580 west, continue straight at it becomes S.R. 584. After about two miles, road will split. Bear left at S.R. 586/Curlew Road. Follow Curlew for about three miles. Turn right and go north on U.S. 19. Turn left and go west on Klosterman Road. Take the second entrance to the St. Petersburg College Campus on your left.

Pinellas County – West Central Florida

"THIS PLACE
IS AN
ABSOLUTELY
WONDERFUL
SURPRISE."

Packinghouse Art Gallery
CELEBRATE NATURE IN PHOTOGRAPHS

Pinellas County – West Central Florida

Packinghouse Art Gallery

Spacious display space provides a rich array of photographs of nature.

A beautiful woodcarving of a bird frozen in flight.

Packinghouse Art Gallery

The Trip

Photography is transformed into beautiful art at this Pinellas County gallery. You'll find more than 4,000 square feet of space dedicated to photography in a building that was once a citrus packinghouse. Built in 1925, this building now houses a display of photographs of nature from throughout Florida and the world.

What To See

I was amazed to see that many of these pictures look more like oil paintings than photographs. Every direction you turn, you'll find precious moments caught in time. From an Eastern Swallowtail sitting on an iris, to a hummingbird caught in mid-flight, these stunning photos are truly a treat for your eyes. The recently renovated gallery has a new exhibition about every three months. The work of Arthur Morris, the most published bird photographer in the U.S., is a highlight of the display.

Other Highlights

About half of the space in the gallery is filled with exhibitions. The rest is devoted to a photography studio, classroom space and a multipurpose room for professional photographers. Custom framing is also available.

10900 OAKHURST ROAD LARGO, FL 33774 (727) 596-7822

Admission: *Free*

Hours: *Open Monday through Saturday, 10 a.m. to 5 p.m. Closed Sunday and major holidays.*

www.packinghousegallery.com

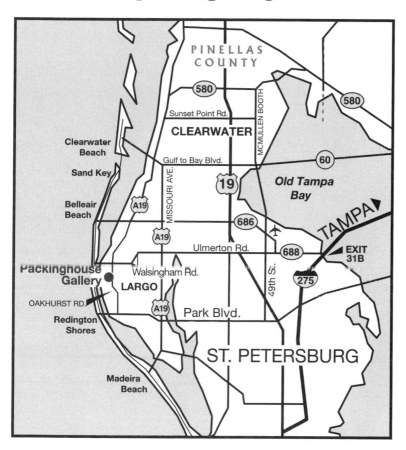

Directions

From Tampa, take Interstate 275 south toward St. Petersburg. Take Ulmerton Road/S.R. 688 west (Exit #31B). Continue on Ulmerton Road to Oakhurst Road, about 12.5 miles from the interstate exit. Turn left and go south on Oakhurst. The gallery about one-half mile farther on the right.

"Precious Moments Caught in Time."

St. Petersburg Museum Of History

WHERE HISTORY LIVES AND TAKES FLIGHT

Pinellas County – West Central Florida

St. Petersburg Museum Of History

Front page history awaits in St. Pete.

St. Petersburg-The Sunshine City

St. Petersburg Museum Of History

The Trip

Your imagination takes flight as you enter this tribute to St. Petersburg's historic past. A new exhibit celebrating the history of the city is one of the highlights of this "One Tank Trip."

What To See

One of the centerpieces of the museum is an antique aircraft called the "Benoist." It's a working replica of the craft that flew the world's first scheduled commercial flight. On Jan. 1, 1914, a young pilot by the name of Tony Jannus flew across Tampa Bay carrying one passenger, some freight and mail. The rest, as they say, "is history." Another area of interest pays tribute to the grand hotels of the city's past and present. The galleries contain many popular icons that symbolize this area. The most famous is one of the green benches, a symbol of the slower pace of life along Central Avenue. Be sure to take a seat and soak in the past.

Other Highlights

You'll find a small gift shop inside for souvenirs, postcards and a few "artsy" gifts. Be sure to take a stroll outside the museum as well. If you're up for it, venture down to The Pier and enjoy the view.

335 2ND AVENUE NE
ST. PETERSBURG, FL 33701
(727) 894-1052

Admission: *$7 for adults, $5 for seniors (60+), $3 for students and children 7-17, free for children under 6.*

Hours: *Monday through Saturday, 10 a.m. to 5 p.m.; Sunday, 1 p.m. to 5 p.m.*

www.stpetemuseumofhistory.org

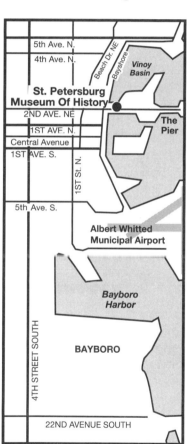

Directions

From Tampa, take Interstate 275 south to St. Petersburg. Take The Pier Exit (Exit #23A) and follow I-375 to 4th Street North. Turn right. Go two blocks to 2nd Avenue North. Turn left. Museum is on the left side of approach to The Pier.

"MANY POPULAR ICONS FROM ST. PETERSBURG'S PAST."

Science Center Of Pinellas County
A PLACE FOR STUDENTS OF LIFE

Pinellas County – West Central Florida

Science Center Of Pinellas County

The Planetarium invites visitors to look to the stars.

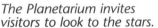

Science Center Of Pinellas County

Visitors can enjoy animals up close and personal in the touch tank.

The Trip
If you're looking for a place to take the kids that's fun and educational, head straight to the Science Center of Pinellas County. Every corner of this great facility has something to offer.

What To See
Would you like to travel to the stars? How about spending a few minutes on the moon and Mars? The center's planetarium is incredible with state-of-the-art technology that will take you out of this world. If you're ready for the deep sea after your deep space journey, visit the marine room. You can actually reach out and touch some of the animals swimming in the big tank. From there, step back in time and experience 16th century Florida in a Native American Village. Among the highlights, a chief's mound and temple, a village cook's hut, and a realistic archaeological excavation. There's so much more, but you get the idea!

Other Highlights
There's a huge telescope that you can gaze through during one of the center's star parties at night. Call ahead for days and times. Speaking of parties, you can arrange to have your child's birthday party on-site here. If you need a quick gift for your little one, take a walk through the gift shop.

7701 22ND AVENUE N.
ST. PETERSBURG, FL 33710
(727) 384-0027

Admission: Monday through Friday, $1; Saturday, $5.

Hours: August through June: Monday through Friday, 9 a.m. to 4 p.m.; Saturday, year-round, 10 a.m. to 4 p.m. Closed Sunday and major holidays.

www.sciencecenterofpinellas.com

Directions

From Tampa, take Interstate 275 south to St. Petersburg. At 22nd Avenue North (Exit #24) turn right and go west. Continue for nearly 10 miles. Center is four blocks west of Tyrone Square Mall.

"SCIENCE AND FUN– UNDER THE SAME ROOF."

Weedon Island Preserve
WHERE EARLY RESIDENTS MADE THEIR MARK

Pinellas County – West Central Florida

Nature in all its wild glory is on display, often seeming to pose for visitors.

Weedon Island Preserve

A high view of the preserve shows land and water in eternal partnership.

The Trip

One of the best parts of this "One Tank" business is when you come upon a jewel. Welcome to Pinellas County's Weedon Island Preserve on Old Tampa Bay. Tucked away between Tampa and St. Petersburg, this 3,164-acre gem is a celebration of mangrove forests, salt flats, pine flatwoods and oak hammocks.

What To See

People lived on this island hundreds of years ago, long before there were paved roads and tourists. Ample evidence of the early residents can be found in the education center. You'll see everything from arrowheads to pottery shards. The preserve was also once used as a landing field for early airplanes. Parts of the new cultural and natural history center are works in progress. You'll find display cases, old photographs and interactive exhibits.

Other Highlights

Outside, the preserve offers miles of hiking trails and a boardwalk that meanders through salt flats and mangroves. Nature in all its wild glory is on display, often seeming to pose for visitors. If you're up to it, climb to the top of the 47-foot observation tower and take in the spectacular view. Below, you'll see some of the several miles of canoe trails that are also available to enjoy. There's even a fishing pier at the preserve for all you anglers.

1800 WEEDON DRIVE NE
ST. PETERSBURG, FL 33702
(727) 453-6500

T R I P
43

Admission: *Free*

Hours: *Preserve is open dawn to dusk daily all year. The education center is open Wednesday through Sunday, 10 a.m. to 4 p.m. Closed Monday and Tuesday.*

www.weedonislandcenter.org

Directions

From Tampa, take Interstate 275 south to Gandy Boulevard (Exit #28). Turn left and go east on Gandy. Go approximately one mile then turn right and go south on San Martin Boulevard. Drive approximately one mile and turn left onto Weedon Drive. Follow this road directly to the entrance to the preserve.

"A CELEBRATION OF MANGROVE FOREST, SALT FLATS, PINE FLATWOODS AND OAK HAMMOCKS."

Pinellas County – West Central Florida

Weedon Island Preserve

World Of Disc Golf
A DIFFERENT KIND OF GOLF GAME

Pinellas County – West Central Florida

Going for par.

Teeing off at hole #10. Watch out for the water!

The Trip

Playing disc golf is a unique and fun way to spend a day. After hearing a lot of talk about this recreational sport born out of the world of Frisbees, I decided to give it a try. I'm glad I did.

What To See

There is an ever expanding number of dedicated disc golf courses across the country and many of them are in Florida and the Bay Area. We traveled to beautiful Cliff Stevens Park in Clearwater. Twenty-one holes, mostly par 3s, await. The discs you use look like small frisbees. Some are drivers, some are putters, and some are mid-range. You can buy them at many sporting goods stores. Like the little white ball variety, this game takes little time to learn but a lifetime to perfect. In the picture above, you can see me "putting" into the basket. By the way, I missed!

Other Highlights

Most, if not all, of the courses have trees and water and are very scenic. Enjoy the sights! And if you see some kids in scuba gear, don't be surprised. They may try and sell you some used discs that they have retrieved in the water hazards. The web site addresses on the right will help you locate the courses.

CLIFF STEPHENS PARK
901 FAIRWOOD AVE.
CLEARWATER, FL 33755
(727) 562-4800

Admission: *Free (BYOD: Bring Your Own Discs.)*

Hours: *Open dawn to dusk.*

www.tbdsc.com
www.pdga.com/course

Directions
From Tampa, take S.R. 60 (Courtney Campbell Causeway) west. Continue on the causeway when it becomes Gulf-to-Bay Boulevard. Turn right and go north on McMullen Booth Road. Turn left and go west on Drew Street. Then turn right on Fairwood Avenue. Follow road around course. Entrance is on the right.

"THIS IS THE SPORTS RAGE OF THE FUTURE. TRUST ME!"

DeSoto National Memorial

A BEAUTIFUL NATIONAL TREASURE

Manatee County – West Central Florida

The Spanish Conquistadors paid this part of Florida an early visit 500 years ago.

National Park Service

National Park Service

Reenactments are staged to suggest how this part of the New World was visited by Hernando DeSoto and his men.

The Trip

A history lesson almost 500 hundred years old can be found in Bradenton at the DeSoto National Memorial. A national park, the memorial is located at the mouth of the Manatee River at the southern end of Tampa Bay.

What To See

With the Gulf of Mexico about 5 miles to the west, there is a historical memorial to the Spanish explorer Hernando DeSoto. This national park commemorates the often brutal expedition and legacy of DeSoto and his Spanish Conquistadors. At the visitor's center, you'll find interesting displays and a good selection of books and souvenirs. There is also a theater where you can sit and enjoy a 22-minute movie depicting the events that happened here more than 500 years ago. The beautiful setting outside also includes some remarkable West Indian birch trees and a half-mile nature trail.

Other Highlights

During certain times of the year, you can be treated to a reenactment of DeSoto's first encounter with Native Americans. Call ahead for living history dates and times.

END OF 75TH STREET NW
BRADENTON, FL
(941) 792-0458

Admission: *Free*

Hours: *Open dawn to dusk. If staying after 5 p.m., visitors must park outside gates.*

www.nps.gov/deso

Directions

From Tampa, take Interstate 75 south to S.R. 64/Manatee Avenue (Exit #220). Turn right and go west through Bradenton. Turn right and go north on 75th Street NW. Continue for about 2 miles. Road will lead into park.

"A LIVING HISTORY JUST DOWN THE ROAD."

Manatee Village Historical Park

TIME TRAVEL TO OLD FLORIDA

Manatee County – West Central Florida

Manatee Village Historical Park

The Manatee County's first courthouse, dating from 1860. It was moved here in 1976.

The Old Settler's House is a typical farmhouse from pioneer Florida.

Manatee Village Historical Park

The Trip

Travel back in time for a glimpse of what life was like in Old Florida. This Bradenton-based "One Tank" takes you back to the days of one-room schoolhouses and outdoor plumbing.

What To See

Established in 1976 to preserve the area's history, this classic turn of the century village tells a story of days gone by. A "Cracker Gothic" style house should be one of your first stops. Outside, if you're thirsty, you can pump cool water from the well. For some laughs, don't miss the two-seater outhouse. The K.W. Wiggins store should be next on your list of things to see. The brick building is more than 100 years old and was a gathering spot for the community to catch up on the news and stock up on supplies. You can also explore Manatee County's first courthouse. Built in 1860, it's the oldest courthouse in the state. There's even an old ballot box out back.

Other Highlights

If you're interested, you can view the Manatee Burying Ground where many pioneers from this area were laid to rest. Ask for the gate key at the park office located on the second floor of the Wiggins store. The cemetery is across the street from the park along 15th Street East.

604 15TH STREET E.
BRADENTON, FL 34208
(941) 749-7165

Admission: *Free Donations accepted.*

Hours: *Open Monday through Friday, 9 a.m. to 4:30 p.m.; Sunday, 1:30 p.m. to 4:30 p.m. Closed Saturday. Closed on weekends in July and August.*

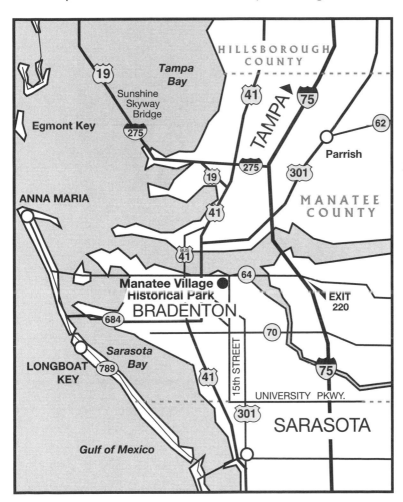

Directions
From Tampa, take Interstate 75 south to S.R. 64/Manatee Avenue (Exit #220). Turn right and go west through Bradenton. Go to 15th Street East. Village is at intersection, on your left.

"BUILDINGS
THAT TELL
THE STORY
OF DAYS
GONE BY."

Sea Hagg
Nautical Oddities

SEE THE SEA HAGG
DOWN BY THE SEASHORE

Manatee County – West Central Florida

Sea Hagg Nautical Oddities

There's a rustic fishing village look to this collection of antiques.

A beautiful example of what you'll find.

Sea Hagg Nautical Oddities

The Trip

There's a place I found that is a treasure trove of discoveries from the sea and shore. The shop is located in Cortez, a quaint fishing village in Manatee County.

What To See

You can spend hours here just looking at all of the antiques, nautical oddities and curiosities on the walls, in the corners and hanging from the ceiling. New items are being added almost daily, giving the impression of an over-stuffed closet. In fact, the stock room in back was such an alluring place that customers kept straining to look inside. The owners finally had to open it to the public. In addition, there are the "sea haggs" themselves, everywhere you look. These custom-made, one-of-a-kind female figurines come in all shapes and sizes, some small and some quite big. They're crafted from all sorts of materials — woods, metals and ceramics — and often people just drop by to see the latest creations.

Other Highlights

Don't overlook "The Phish Emporium," a shack right across the street. After the Sea Hagg became too loaded with stuff, the shack was born, and it quickly filled with even more stuff. If there's something nautical you're seeking for that special person or for that empty spot in your home, give them a call. Collectors of old fishing lures especially like to go "phishing" here.

12304 CORTEZ ROAD W.
CORTEZ, FL 34215
(941) 795-5756

Manatee County – West Central Florida

Admission: *Free*

Hours: *Monday through Friday, 9:30 a.m. to 5:30 p.m.; Saturday, 10 a.m. to 5 p.m.; Sunday, by appointment only.*

www.seahagg.com

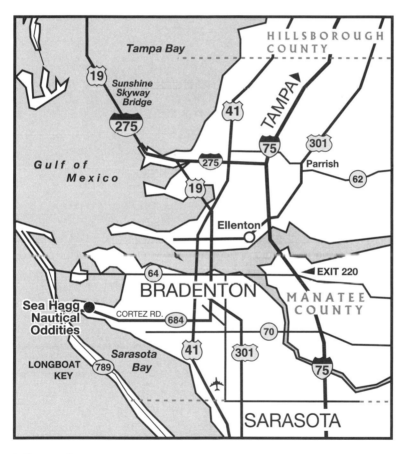

Directions

From Tampa, take Interstate 75 south to S.R. 64/Manatee Avenue (Exit #220). Turn right and go west to U.S. 41. Turn left and go south on U.S. 41. Turn right and go west on Cortez Road/S.R. 684. Store is at the intersection of Cortez Road and 123rd Street, on the right.

"A 'TREASURE TROVE' OF DISCOVERIES."

Village Of The Arts
A VERY ARTSY WALK-ABOUT

A stroll among Bradenton's art galleries yields art work inside and out.

The Trip
We're off to a pretty little neighborhood where you can never, ever be too "artsy." Artists of all disciplines live, work and sell their wares in this quaint, picturesque showplace that is the crown jewel of downtown Bradenton. More than 30 artists-in-residence galleries make up this "Village of the Arts." They show their talent off in the twice a month "Artwalk," all within walking distance from downtown Bradenton.

What To See
The artists' galleries are lined up side by side in their neighborhood. The big party takes place the first and second Friday and Saturday of each month. As you stroll in and out of the various galleries gazing at the artwork, you'll often meet the artists themselves. Some of them even offer complimentary snacks. You'll get the chance to fill your senses with the arts and tickle your taste buds.

Other Highlights
Some artists' galleries are also their homes, providing an even more intimate look at the creative environment. If you can't make the "Artwalk," you'll still find other galleries and shops to enjoy. Many are open daily, especially during tourist season.

VILLAGE OF THE ARTS
DOWNTOWN BRADENTON
BRADENTON, FL 34205
(941) 747-8056

Admission: Free

Hours: First and Second Friday of each month, 6:30 p.m. to 10 p.m. First and second Saturday of each month, 11 a.m. to 4 p.m. Many shops open daily.

www.villageofthearts.com

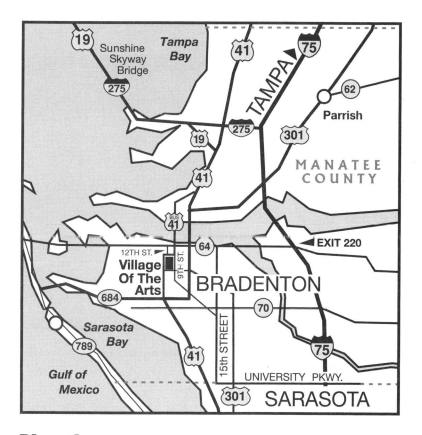

Directions

From Tampa, take Interstate 75 south to S.R. 64/Manatee Avenue (Exit #220). Turn right and go west on S.R. 64 through Bradenton. Turn left at 12 Street W. Then left and a quick right into village. Parking on the street. Some galleries have parking lots.

"FILL YOUR SENSES WITH THE ARTS AND TICKLE YOUR TASTEBUDS."

Pelican Man Bird Sanctuary
A HERO AND HIS SANCTUARY

Sarasota County – West Central Florida

Pelican Man Bird Sanctuary

Some pelicans come just for a few days and a drink of water.

Pelicans by the thousands have called this place home.

Pelican Man Bird Sanctuary

The Trip

This is a remarkable place founded by a remarkable man. Dale Shields, known as "The Pelican Man," passed away in January 2003, but his incredible bird sanctuary lives on. It is the largest wildlife rescue and rehab center in Florida. Dale was recognized for his work by many people, including President George Bush who designated Shields as the "184th point of light" in 1990. "The Pelican Man" was the only person ever to receive that award for his work on behalf of animals.

What To See

There are 55 different species of Florida birds here, as well as other rescued animals. Since its founding in 1981, thousands of birds have been healed and released back into the wild. Be sure to stop by and see "Liberty," a bald eagle who years ago was rescued after being hit by a car. He can no longer fly, so this is home. Look for "Angie," a crow who loves to lament, "No fair!"

Other Highlights

Don't be afraid to ask questions of the volunteers who are always on hand to educate and inform the public. The sanctuary's volunteers drive more than 150,000 miles a year responding to approximately 6,000 rescue calls, so they have lots of stories to share. There is an opportunity to "adopt a bird" with an annual donation. Just ask one of the volunteers. You can also explore the natural beauty of Sarasota Bay on a two-hour educational boat tour.

1708 KEN THOMPSON PARKWAY
SARASOTA, FL 34236
(941) 388-4444

Admission: *$6 for adults; $4 for children.*

Hours: *Open daily 10 a.m. to 5 p.m. Closed Thanksgiving, Christmas and New Year's Day.*

www.pelicanman.org

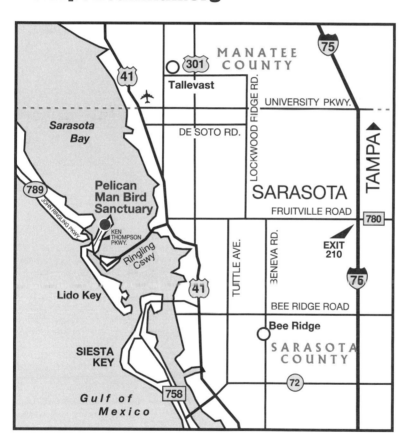

Directions

From Tampa, take Interstate 75 south to Sarasota. At S.R. 780/Fruitville Road (Exit #210) turn right and go west. Take Fruitville to U.S. 41. Turn left and then take a right on John Ringling Causeway. Just before the Longboat Key Bridge, look for sign on the right for Mote Marine Laboratory and Pelican Man Bird Sanctuary (Ken Thompson Parkway). Turn right. They share a parking lot.

"A HERO'S
SANCTUARY
LIVES ON."

Sarasota
Ever-Glides Tour

SEEING SARASOTA ON TWO WHEELS

You can glide almost forever on an Ever-Glide.

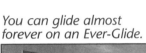

Sarasota Ever-Glides

Leading the way on a two-wheel tour in Sarasota.

The Trip

Get ready to roll on an exciting 21st century adventure. This "One Tank" is by far the most unique trip in the book. You will get to climb aboard a "Segway Human Transporter." The makers of this newfangled, two-wheeled personal vehicle say it will revolutionize pedestrian transportation. To me, it was just plain fun!

What To See

After some basic instruction on how to operate the Segway, you'll take a brief "test drive" in a training area. The self-balancing machine responds to the lean of your body. Once on board, the first minute or two may seem a bit weird, but it's amazing how quickly you'll figure these things out. It goes forward when you lean forward and slows down when you lean back. Before you know it, you'll be ready to step up and head out on your guided tour. The two-and-a-half-hour experience includes a visit to historic parts of the city, including homes built in the 1920s and '30s. The highlight of the tour is rolling along Sarasota's beautiful waterfront.

Other Highlights

The tour includes a snack and a drink. There are also special dinner and sunset tours, which are especially popular in the summertime.

200 S. WASHINGTON BLVD., #11
SARASOTA, FL 34236
(941) 363-9556

Admission: *Two-and-a-half-hour, six-mile guided tour is $59 per person. Ages 12-80+.*

Hours: *Call for details. Reservations required. Maximum of 9 riders per tour. Morning and afternoon tours available seven days a week.*

www.floridaever-glides.com

Directions
From Tampa, take Interstate 75 south to Sarasota. At S.R. 780/Fruitville Road (Exit #210) turn right and go west. Take Fruitville west about six miles to U.S. 301 (Washington Boulevard). Turn left and go south three blocks. Turn right onto Adams Lane. Florida Ever-Glides is on the northwest corner of Adams Lane and Washington Boulevard.

"A GENUINE 21ST CENTURY 'ONE TANK TRIP'."

The Teddy Bear Museum

A PLACE THAT BEARS VISITING

Southeast Florida

Teddy Bears abound in this museum.

Teddy Bear Museum

There are old teddy bears, handmade teddy bears and just plain huggable teddy bears from all over the world.

Teddy Bear Museum

The Trip

A dream home for teddy bears! Welcome to cuddly bear heaven, the Teddy Bear Museum. It is the first of its kind in the world and the only one in North America.

What To See

The collections started in 1984 when Frances Pew Hayes received a Christmas present from her 5-year-old grandson, an M&M bear he got by mailing in his empty M&M candy packets. It was her first teddy, but far from her last. For some reason, she received nothing but bears as gifts. Her collection has fostered this museum, which owns more than 15,000 bears. At least one-third are on display at any one time. While they're all special, be sure to look for Bear No. 1, the very first bear registered in the museum's collection. And don't forget to enjoy the museum's highly-collectible Steif bears. One bear is more than 100 years old.

Other Highlights

The museum offers several children's programs, lots of reference materials, and even bear-making classes. And before you bid the bears 'bye, stop at the museum gift shop. Plenty of sweetie pies looking for a home. In fact, there's nothing in the gift shop but bears.

2511 PINE RIDGE ROAD
NAPLES, FL 34109
(239) 598-2711

Admission: *$8 for adults, $6 for seniors (60+), $3 for children 4-12, free for children 3 and under.*

Hours: *Open Tuesday through Saturday, 10 a.m. to 5 p.m. Closed Sunday, Monday and major holidays.*

www.teddymuseum.com

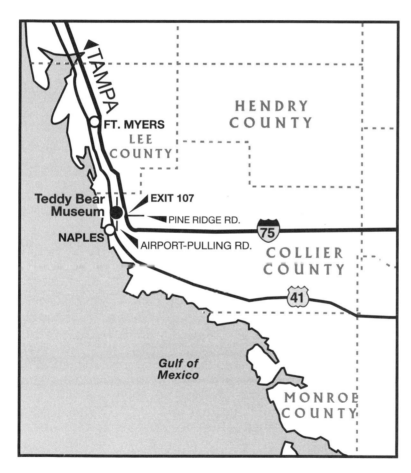

Directions
From Tampa, take Interstate 75 south toward Naples. At Pine Ridge Road (Exit #107) Turn right and go west. Go to Airport-Pulling Road. Museum is on the right at the intersection.

"WELCOME TO CUDDLY BEAR HEAVEN."

Coral Castle
ONE MAN'S TRIBUTE TO HIS LOST LOVE

Southwest Florida

Coral Castle

*A castle of coral—
handmade.*

Coral Castle

Coral Castle

*One man's
homage to
his love leaves
the world with
more questions
than answers.*

The Trip

This "One Tank Trip" is a magical mystery tour to a place where some questions may never be answered. It's a place one man built to honor his ex-girlfriend. How he did it is anybody's guess.

What To See

Built over a period of 20 years by Edward Leedskalnin, an immigrant from Latvia, this "castle" is a monument to a lost love. As the story goes, Ed was jilted by his girlfriend on the eve of their wedding. Once settled in the United States, Ed began carving this tribute to his former girlfriend. Working in secret, mostly at night, he never allowed anyone to see how he carved the hard coral rock into the various chairs, tables and monuments that fill the castle. One of the great mysteries is how Ed, who supposedly weighed only 100 pounds, managed to raise and position massive coral blocks into place. Some of them weighed more than 25 tons! Altogether, Ed quarried and sculpted more than 1,100 tons of coral rock for his castle, using tools fashioned from auto junkyard parts.

Other Highlights

In addition to admiring the construction of the eight-foot-high walls, check out some of the very creative furniture Ed made. There's a coral rocking chair that weighs thousands of pounds, yet moves with the touch of a finger. There's also Ed's creation of a 5,000-pound, heart-shaped coral rock table with a red blooming ixora growing from its center. According to Ripley's "Believe It Or Not," it's the world's largest Valentine.

28655 S. DIXIE HIGHWAY
HOMESTEAD, FL 33033
(305) 248-6345

Admission: *$9.75 for adults; $6.50 for seniors; $5 for children 7-12.*

Hours: *Open daily 8 a.m. to 6 p.m.*

www.coralcastle.com

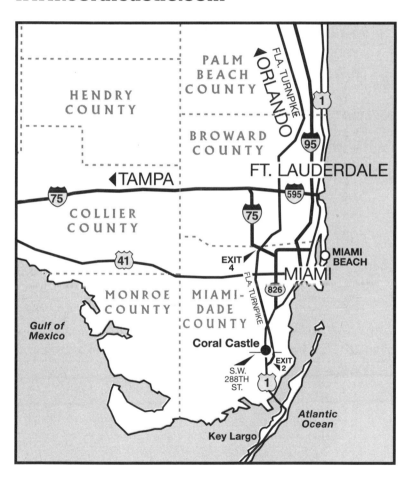

Directions

From Tampa, take Interstate 75 south toward Miami. Take Exit #4 and go south on S.R. 821/Florida Turnpike toward Homestead. Take the Campbell Drive (Exit #2) and go west to U.S. 1. Turn right and go north to 288th Street. Castle is located at that intersection.

"A MAN'S HEART IS HIS CASTLE."

Weather Guide

	Fort Myers		Jacksonville		Key West		Miami	
	High/Low	Rainfall	High/Low	Rainfall	High/Low	Rainfall	High/Low	Rainfall
January	74°/53°	1.8"	64°/42°	3.3"	75°/65°	2.0"	75°/59°	2.0"
February	76°/54°	2.2"	67°/44°	3.9"	75°/65°	1.8"	76°/60°	2.1"
March	80°/59°	3.1"	74°/50°	3.7"	79°/69°	1.7"	79°/64°	2.4"
April	85°/62°	1.1"	80°/56°	2.8"	82°/72°	1.8"	83°/68°	3.0"
May	89°/68°	3.9"	85°/63°	3.6"	85°/76°	3.5"	85°/72°	6.2"
June	91°/73°	9.5"	89°/70°	5.7"	88°/79°	5.1"	88°/75°	9.3"
July	91°/75°	8.3"	92°/73°	5.6"	89°/80°	3.6"	89°/77°	5.7"
August	91°/75°	9.7"	91°/72°	7.9"	89°/79°	5.0"	89°/77°	7.6"
September	90°/74°	7.8"	87°/70°	7.1"	88°/79°	5.9"	88°/76°	7.6"
October	86°/69°	2.9"	80°/60°	2.9"	84°/76°	4.4"	85°/72°	5.6"
November	81°/61°	1.6"	73°/50°	2.2"	80°/71°	2.8"	80°/67°	2.7"
December	76°/55°	1.6"	67°/44°	2.7"	76°/67°	2.0"	77°/62°	1.8"

	Orlando		Pensacola		Tampa Bay		Tallahassee	
	High/Low	Rainfall	High/Low	Rainfall	High/Low	Rainfall	High/Low	Rainfall
January	72°/51°	2.3"	60°/41°	4.7"	70°/49°	2.0"	63°/38°	4.8"
February	72°/50°	4.0"	63°/44°	5.4"	71°/51°	3.1"	66°/40°	5.5"
March	78°/56°	3.2"	69°/51°	5.7"	77°/56°	3.0"	73°/47°	6.2"
April	84°/61°	1.3"	76°/58°	3.4"	82°/61°	1.2"	80°/52°	3.7"
May	88°/67°	3.1"	83°/66°	4.2"	87°/67°	3.1"	86°/61°	4.8"
June	91°/72°	7.5"	89°/72°	6.4"	90°/73°	5.5"	91°/68°	6.9"
July	92°/74°	7.2"	90°/74°	7.4"	90°/74°	6.6"	91°/71°	8.8"
August	91°/74°	7.1"	89°/74°	7.3"	90°/74°	7.6"	91°/71°	7.5"
September	89°/73°	6.3"	86°/70°	5.4"	89°/73°	6.0"	88°/68°	5.6"
October	84°/67°	2.9"	79°/60°	4.1"	84°/65°	2.0"	81°/56°	2.9"
November	77°/57°	1.7"	70°/51°	3.5"	78°/57°	1.8"	73°/46°	3.9"
December	73°/52°	2.0"	63°/44°	4.3"	72°/52°	2.2"	66°/41°	5.0"

About Florida Weather

As you plan your **One Tank Trips"** across Florida, I thought you would like to get a general feel for our weather. Check out the accompanying charts which will give you an overview of our weather.

There are many reasons why Florida is a destination state. Number one on most lists is the delightful weather! As a rule, Florida weather is pleasant with mild winters and hot summers. Summer thunderstorms, though sometimes severe, are usually short-lived and provide a break from the afternoon heat. As you travel, remember your sunscreen. Also, keep an eye on the sky. Thunderstorms build quickly during the summer time and it is important to respect the danger of lightning. Hurricane season begins in June and runs through the end of November. If you are in an area in which a hurricane is approaching, tune in to **FOX13** to keep abreast of the warnings.

You can track hurricanes and check the daily weather by logging on to **www.wtvt.com**. We also have a link to SkyTower Radar, the most powerful Doppler radar in Florida.

Here's wishing you a great time as you travel across our great state.

Paul Dellegatto
WTVT FOX13 Chief Meteorologist

About Florida Sports

Sports is a passion not a pastime in Florida. Our state is home to eleven professional sports franchises, so you can see how those of us who live in the Sunshine State enjoy our sports.

The listings here are more than just sports spots. These are destinations that many families, including my own, have enjoyed.

As Sports Director for **FOX13**, I enjoy the professional and personal experiences working and living in Florida provide. Our lists covers everything from NFL football to NASCAR.

Chip Carter
WTVT FOX13 Sports Director

FLORIDA SPORTS ATTRACTIONS

National Football League
Tampa Bay Buccaneers, Raymond James Stadium, Tampa
Jacksonville Jaguars, Alltel Stadium, Jacksonville
Miami Dolphins, Pro Player Stadium, Fort Lauderdale

Major League Baseball
Tampa Bay Devil Rays, Tropicana Field, St. Petersburg
Florida Marlins, Pro Player Stadium, Fort Lauderdale

National Hockey League
Tampa Bay Lightning, St. Pete Times Forum, Tampa
Florida Panthers, National Car Rental Center, Miami

National Basketball Association
Miami Heat, American Airlines Arena, Miami
Orlando Magic, TD Waterhouse Centre, Orlando

Arena Football League
Tampa Bay Storm, St. Pete Times Forum, Tampa
Orlando Predators, TD Waterhouse Centre, Orlando

Grapefruit League Spring Training
Atlanta Braves, Disney's Wide World of Sports, Kissimmee
Baltimore Orioles, Fort Lauderdale Stadium, Fort Lauderdale
Boston Red Sox, City of Palms Park, Fort Myers
Cincinnati Reds, Ed Smith Stadium, Sarasota
Cleveland Indians, Chain of Lakes Park, Winter Haven
Detroit Tigers, Joker Marchant Stadium, Lakeland
Florida Marlins, Roger Dean Stadium, Jupiter
Houston Astros, Osceola County Stadium, Kissimmee
Los Angeles Dodgers, Vero Beach
Minnesota Twins, Hammond Stadium, Ft. Myers
New York Mets, Tradition Field, Port St. Lucie
New York Yankees, Legends Field, Tampa
Philadelphia Phillies, Bright House Networks Field, Clearwater
Pittsburgh Pirates, McKechnie Field, Bradenton
St. Louis Cardinals, Roger Dean Stadium, Jupiter
Tampa Bay Devil Rays, Progress Energy Park, St. Petersburg
Texas Rangers, Charlotte County Stadium, Port Charlotte
Toronto Blue Jays, Dunedin Stadium, Dunedin

Motorsports
Daytona International Speedway, Daytona Beach
Homestead-Miami Speedway, Homestead
Sebring International Raceway, Sebring
USA International Speedway, Lakeland
Moroso Motorsports Park, Palm Beach Gardens

Colleges & Universities
Bethune-Cookman University, Daytona Beach
University of Central Florida, Orlando
Eckerd College, St. Petersburg
Florida Southern College, Lakeland
University of Florida, Gainesville
Florida A&M University, Tallahassee
Florida State University, Tallahassee
Jacksonville University, Jacksonville
University of Miami, Coral Gables
Rollins College, Winter Park
St. Leo University, St. Leo
University of South Florida, Tampa
University of Tampa, Tampa

Thoroughbred Horse Racing
Calder Race Course, Miami
Gulfstream Park, Hallendale
Hialeah Park, Miami
Pompano Park, Pompano Park
Tampa Bay Downs, Oldsmar

Index

Trip Notes

Trip Notes